MW01284062

FROM PROMPT TO PROFIT

THE MSP PLAYBOOK FOR AI-DRIVEN CLIENT SUCCESS

ART GROSS

Copyright © 2025 Art Gross
All rights reserved.

ISBN: 978-1-64649-503-0 (paperback)
ISBN: 978-1-64649-504-7 (ebook)

No part of this publication may be reproduced, distributed, or transmitted in any form or by any means, including photocopying, recording, or other electronic or mechanical methods, without the prior written permission of the publisher, except in the case of brief quotations embodied in critical reviews and certain other noncommercial uses permitted by copyright law.

CONTENTS

PREFACE

If you're an MSP reading this, you've likely already heard the buzz: "AI is coming."

Actually—AI is already here. And just like with the rise of the internet, cloud computing, HIPAA, and cybersecurity, your clients aren't ready for what's next. But that's exactly why they need you.

I've spent over 25 years running a successful MSP, supporting some of the largest fertility practices in the world. I've helped hundreds of small businesses adopt the internet, install firewalls, move to the cloud, and navigate cybersecurity and compliance.

In 2010, I shouted "HIPAA is coming."

In 2015, I shouted "Cybersecurity is coming."

And now, in 2025, I'm shouting:

"AI is coming, adoption is accelerating—and this time, the change is going to happen faster than any of us expect."

I am not only an MSP but I am also the CEO of Breach Secure Now (BSN). BSN is a platform supporting 3,000 MSPs and 35,000 SMB clients, training over 1 million employees in security, Microsoft 365, and now AI Awareness.

I've seen firsthand how quickly AI adoption is accelerating. But most MSPs still aren't sure what to do with AI. They're not sure how to make money from it, how to support it, or even how to talk about it with clients.

This book changes that.

It's not a technical deep dive. You won't find complex code, agent architecture, or academic AI theory. Instead, you'll find a field guide... a practical playbook and a blueprint for how to:

- Start using AI in your own MSP
- Help your clients adopt AI safely
- Turn training into your modern trojan horse
- Build recurring services around real-world use cases
- Avoid getting displaced by AI consultants or other third parties

I wrote this book because I believe MSPs have the single greatest opportunity since the cloud and cybersecurity to redefine their value to clients.

AI will become infrastructure.

MSPs are the natural stewards of infrastructure.

This is your moment.

Let's make sure you don't miss it.

—**Art**

1

THE NEXT WAVE IS HERE

I've been around long enough to see technology change everything—more than once.

In 1984, I was a computer science major at Penn State University and an intern at Merck & Co., Inc., when the IBM PC had just launched. My job? Help roll out the first desktop computers. A few years later I helped connect these PCs to Merck's brand-new token ring network. In the mid-1990s, I was part of the team that put Merck.com on the internet. I became one of their first "internet evangelists," flying around the world explaining what this new thing called the internet could do.

It felt like magic. And most people didn't believe it would matter.

Then I left Merck, in 2000, to start my own IT business—what we now call an MSP. During these 25 years, I have helped businesses adopt every new technology wave from the internet to email, to the cloud, to cybersecurity, and compliance.

In 2010, when HIPAA regulations ramped up, I saw the opportunity and started HIPAA Secure Now, a company to help medical practices become compliant. I was shouting, "HIPAA is coming!"

By 2015, cybercrime exploded. Ransomware crippled small businesses, MSPs were getting breached, and employees had zero training. I saw the gap again and built Breach Secure Now to deliver security awareness training to SMB employees. Once again I was shouting, this time, "Cybersecurity is coming!"

And today, I'm telling you this:

AI is the next wave. And this time, it's coming faster than all the others combined.

What Makes This Wave Different?

AI isn't just one tool. It's not one platform, one device, one regulatory requirement. It's a new layer of productivity.

Like the internet made businesses connected, and the cloud made businesses mobile, and cybersecurity made businesses resilient, AI will make businesses exponentially more capable.

Each wave built on the last.

Each one transformed how work gets done.

But AI? AI accelerates everything.

This isn't hype. This is history repeating itself, with more urgency.

Unlike those earlier waves, AI tools are easy to access. Employees can use them today. Some already are. And that means your clients are already adopting AI—without you.

They're copying sensitive data into ChatGPT.

They're installing browser extensions that integrate with internal systems.

They're trusting AI outputs without verification.

They're skipping past IT altogether.

Sound familiar? It should. This is what shadow IT looked like in 2012. And just like then, it's happening because MSPs haven't stepped in yet.

The AI Gap Is Your Opportunity

Most SMBs are flying blind. They have no AI policies. No employee training. They don't understand the risks. They don't know where to start. And they aren't asking for help. Yet.

But they will.

And the MSPs who are ready—those who have their own internal use cases, client-facing training, and a basic AI services stack—will win.

I wrote this book to help MSPs win!

The Opportunity Is Bigger Than You Think

Let's put it in perspective. Cybersecurity became a massive revenue stream for MSPs. So did cloud services. But those shifts took years to materialize.

AI is moving faster. The tools are consumer-grade. The pressure is internal because employees are driving it. The benefits are immediate and measurable. And the risk of ignoring it? Catastrophic.

We've already seen companies leak data, trust hallucinated AI answers, and get phished by AI-generated emails. That's not theoretical. That's happening in SMBs right now.

This is your chance to help your clients adopt AI safely, effectively, and with structure. In the process, you can build a new layer of services for your business.

This Is Your Netscape Moment

In 1994, Netscape launched its browser and made the internet real for the average user. That launch created millions of jobs, billions of dollars, and a new way of working.

AI is our Netscape moment.

The Bottom Line

Right now, every MSP has a choice with AI.

>...You can ignore it and fall behind—pretend it's not happening while your clients adopt tools without guidance or policies.

>...You can watch it and play catch-up. Wait for the market to mature. Let others make the mistakes. Then scramble to offer services when clients are already asking why you're late to the game.

>...Or you can lead it and grow. Start the conversations now. Build the expertise today. Be the trusted advisor when clients need guidance most.

I'm rooting for your MSP. And hopefully this book will arm you with the information you need to lead.

You don't need to be an expert.

You don't need to know how to build a GPT or train a model.

You just need to take the first step—and bring your clients with you.

2

TECHNICAL FOUNDATIONS

What You Actually Need to Know

(And What You Don't)

Normally, you would expect a foundations chapter to include a technical deep dive, with focus on large language models (LLMs) and machine learning (ML), or maybe robotic process automation (RPA), Model Context Protocol (MCP), Retrieval Augmented Generation (RAG), or fine-tuning models.

But I'm going to skip over all of that.

Because you don't need to know most of it.

Instead, let's focus on the generative AI tools themselves.

Why I'm Skipping the Technical Details

I like to compare AI to cybersecurity.

If I were writing this book 10 years ago about cybersecurity, I would be tempted to talk about the technical details:

- How to exploit vulnerabilities
- How to get a foothold in a network
- How to move laterally
- How to ensure persistence
- The details of command and control (C2)
- Data exfiltration from a network
- The technical aspects of ransomware and encryption methodologies

Honestly, most MSPs only know this at a surface level. Yet they protect clients and implement layers of cybersecurity. But the truth is, MSPs don't need to know this level of detail about cybersecurity.

MSPs rely on channel vendors to help them with most of the deep technical aspects of cybersecurity.

And that's why I'm skipping over the technical details of AI.

You don't need to be an AI engineer.

You need to be an AI *advisor*.

What You Actually Need to Know

So what do you need to know to start building an AI practice and helping clients?

Start with the Tool Landscape

It's easy to focus on Microsoft Copilot because it integrates seamlessly with Microsoft 365, and Microsoft already has a strong hold on your clients' data.

But here's the reality: your clients' employees are probably already using ChatGPT. When you recommend Copilot, they'll ask, "Why can't we just keep using what we already know?"

You need a good answer.

Different tools excel at different tasks. Some are better for writing—like Claude for long-form content or ChatGPT for quick drafts.

Others shine at data analysis. Copilot excels with Excel integration while Perplexity is perfect for research.

Marketing teams might need video tools like Synthesia or Google's Veo3 for content creation.

The key insight: one size doesn't fit all.

Your job isn't to pick the "best" AI tool. It's to match the right tools to your clients' specific needs.

The Tool Evaluation Framework

The best way to understand these tools is to buy licenses and start using them.

Evaluate which tool is:

- Easiest to support?
- Best for writing?
- Best for image creation?
- Best for video?
- Best for data analysis?
- Best for research?

This tool selection and evaluation is a critical aspect of building an AI service. And it's one of the main reasons clients will pay you for your advice.

Your AI Tool Scorecard

For each tool, write down the pros and cons—what works well, what doesn't, and where it falls short.

Document the reporting capabilities because clients will ask who's using what and how much value they're getting.

Track the costs across different versions because AI pricing changes frequently and clients need accurate budget planning.

Map out which features come in each version so you can recommend the right tier without overpaying or under-delivering.

Note integration capabilities with existing client systems. Does it play nice with their CRM, their Microsoft 365 environment, their line-of-business apps?

Finally, document security and compliance considerations, because that's often the first objection clients raise when discussing AI adoption.

This research and insight will be extremely valuable to clients.

Just as you understand the different SKUs and licensing of Microsoft 365, knowing the ins and outs and licensing and capabilities of AI tools is equally important.

Sample Scorecard
July 2025

Tool	Cost & Tiers	Reporting	Integration	Security & Compliance
Chat GPT	Free, Plus $20/mo, Pro $200/mo, Team, Enterprise	Yes (Basic-Advanced)	M365, APIs	SOC2, HIPAA (Enterprise)
Claude	Free, Pro $20/mo, Team $30/user, Enterprise	Yes	Slack, API	SOC2
Gemini	Free, Pro $19.99/mo, Biz/Ent Workspace	Limited	Google Docs, Sheets, Gmail	SOC2, Google Infra
Perplexity	Free, Pro $20/mo	Yes	Browser, API	Unclear
Midjourney	$10-$60/mo (Basic-Mega)	No	Discord only	Unknown
DALL-E	Included in Plus/Team/Ent; $0.02/image (D2)	Yes (via ChatGPT)	ChatGPT APIs	Same as OpenAI
Synthesia	Free, Starter $29/mo, Creator $89/mo, Ent	Yes	CRM, LMS, APIs	GDPR, SOC2
ElevenLabs	Free, Starter $5/mo, up to Enterprise	Yes	API	SOC2
Microsoft Copilot	M365 SKU tiers (Biz Premium/E3/E5)	Yes	Office 365	Full Microsoft compliance

The Big Three: What Most Clients Will Ask About

Microsoft Copilot

- Integrated with M365
- Multiple versions (Copilot Pro, Copilot for M365, etc.)
- Strong enterprise features
- Built-in compliance and security controls
- Familiar licensing model for MSPs

ChatGPT (OpenAI)

- Most recognizable brand
- ChatGPT Plus, Team, and Enterprise versions
- Strong for general writing and research
- Limited enterprise controls in lower tiers
- Employees already using the free version

Google Gemini

- Integrated with Google Workspace
- Strong for research and data analysis
- Strong video creation with Veo3
- Multiple pricing tiers
- Growing enterprise features
- Alternative for non-Microsoft shops

You need to know the basics of all three.

There are also Perplexity Pro, Synthesia, and many others. The more you know the various tools and capabilities, the more of a valuable advisor your MSP can be.

What to Focus On (and what to ignore)

Focus your energy on use cases that help clients get real work done faster.

Understand licensing and pricing models so you can recommend the right tools without breaking budgets.

Know the security and compliance features, because clients will ask about data protection before they'll move forward.

Learn integration capabilities and understand what will work with their existing systems and what won't.

Master reporting and usage analytics so you can prove ROI and track adoption.

Importantly, get comfortable with user management and provisioning because this is where MSPs add real value. Clients don't want to figure out who gets access to what, how to set up SSO, or how to manage licenses across departments. They want someone they trust to handle it properly and securely.

For now, skip the complex stuff. API calls and custom integrations are advanced territory that most SMBs won't need in year one. And fine-tuning and model training? That's data scientist work, not MSP work.

Complex automation workflows can wait until clients first master the basics. Advanced prompt engineering is nice to know but not essential for getting started. As for technical architecture details? Let the vendors handle that.

When evaluating AI tools, keep your evaluation at a high level. You're not looking to do API calls or full-blown automation. You're looking for functionality that you can help clients with like writing emails, doing research, and creating marketing images and videos.

This is about use cases that can help your clients, not about API and Model Context Protocol (MCP) integrations. Advanced functionality can be used later. For now, focus on use cases and how good each tool is in specific situations and industries.

The Reporting Challenge

A key aspect of AI services is reporting on tool usage.

Who's using the tools? How much? Are expensive licenses sitting unused?

This insight is exactly what clients need—and what most MSPs aren't prepared to deliver.

Here's the reality:

ChatGPT for Teams doesn't provide employee utilization statistics. That reporting is reserved for ChatGPT Enterprise (at least at the time of this writing).

Microsoft Copilot gives basic utilization data like last-access times—but not much more.

This creates a problem. Because clients will inevitably ask:

- Who's actually using the tools?
- What are they using them for?
- Are we getting ROI on our investment?
- Which departments are adopting fastest?
- What training gaps do we have?

Understanding what data you can gather, and what you can't, is essential.

It affects which tools you recommend, how you structure contracts, and what expectations you set with clients.

More importantly, it determines whether you can prove the value of AI investments or just hope clients will see it for themselves.

Infrastructure Basics You Need to Know

You don't need to be an AI architect, but you should understand the practical considerations that affect client deployments.

Licensing and Usage

- What usage restrictions exist for each tool and version?
- What happens when employees exceed their allocations?
- How often do usage limits reset?

Access and Compatibility

- Most AI tools run in browsers—but some have dedicated desktop or mobile apps
- Feature sets often differ between web and app versions
- Older browsers may not support all AI tool features
- Extension management becomes a security consideration

Enterprise Integration

- Enterprise versions typically support Single Sign-On (SSO)
- Not all AI tools integrate with all SSO providers
- User management and provisioning vary significantly between tools
- What integrations are available (M365, Google Workspace, Dropbox, Salesforce, etc.)

Security and Compliance

What you need to know:

- Which AI tools are approved for business use
- Data retention policies of each tool
- Where client data goes and residency requirements
- How to prevent sensitive data from being input
- Browser extension risks and monitoring
- Do AI models train on the data employees enter?

- Basic compliance considerations (HIPAA, GDPR, PCI, etc.)

What you don't need to know (at least not in-depth)

- How AI models are trained
- Technical details of data encryption
- Advanced threat modeling
- Custom security implementations

Why this matters

These aren't just technical details, they are business decisions that affect security, compliance, and user adoption.

Your Role as Tool Curator

Think of yourself as the AI tool curator for your clients.

Just like you help them choose between different MDR solutions or backup providers, you'll help them choose between different AI tools.

Your value proposition

- "We've tested these tools so you don't have to."
- "We know which ones work best for your industry and specific departments."
- "We can help you avoid wasting money on the wrong licenses."
- "We'll monitor usage and help you optimize your investment."

Become Your Best Case Study

Step 1: Get licenses for the big three to start (Copilot, ChatGPT, Gemini)

Step 2: Use them daily in your own business operations

Step 3: Document what works, what doesn't, and why

Step 4: Test different use cases across your departments

Step 5: Build your evaluation framework and recommendations

Step 6: Start client conversations armed with real experience

The goal: When clients ask, "How do you use AI?" you'll have stories, not theories.

Your hands-on experience becomes your most powerful sales tool—and the foundation for everything that follows.

I will discuss internal adoption for your MSP more in Chapter 10 (Internal First).

The Bottom Line

Become an expert on understanding the various AI tools and their applications. Don't worry about being an expert on every feature and function. Don't worry about the fringe cases. Focus on the main use cases for various departments such as marketing, sales, finance, operations, and support.

Remember:

- You're an advisor, not an engineer
- Practical knowledge beats theoretical knowledge
- Clients pay for guidance, not complexity
- Start simple, then add complexity as clients mature
- Use the tools yourself first

Just like you became trusted with cybersecurity without becoming a pen tester... you can become trusted with AI without becoming a data scientist.

Focus on what matters. Skip what doesn't.

Help clients win.

3

YOU ALREADY KNOW HOW TO DO THIS

The Microsoft 365 Analogy That Changes Everything

At this point, you might be thinking:

"I've dabbled with AI tools. I've played around. But I still don't feel like an expert. I don't know if I'm ready to talk to clients about AI."

Totally understandable. But here's the good news:

You don't need to be an AI expert.

In fact, you've already been here before. Think About Microsoft 365. You already sell it. You support it. You've built services around it.

But let me ask you this:

- Are you an Excel wizard?
- Can you build complex PivotTables, connect external data sources, and write Python scripts inside spreadsheets?
- Are you formatting Word docs with advanced styles or creating high-end design layouts in PowerPoint?

Probably not. And guess what?

Your clients don't expect you to.

They're not calling you to write their Excel formulas or build PowerPoint decks.

Just like...

They're not going to ask you to write ChatGPT prompts for them.

What You *Are* an Expert In

You know which Microsoft 365 SKU is right for a client.

You understand licensing.

You provision the tools.

You configure security settings.

You provide employee access.

You make sure the environment is safe, backed up, and working.

You provide *training* and *support* so employees can use the tools effectively.

That's it. That's the whole model.

And AI? It works the same way.

Treat AI Like You Treat Microsoft 365

Let's walk through the side-by-side:

Microsoft 365	AI Services
Help pick the right version (Business Standard, E3, etc.)	Help pick the right tools (Copilot, ChatGPT Team, Perplexity Pro)
Understand licensing models	Understand pricing tiers and capabilities
Provision and configure tools	Provision AI accounts, configure privacy settings
Set up secure access	Set guardrails, policies, and permissions
Provide end-user training	Provide AI Awareness Training and prompt libraries
Support employees and answer questions	Support employees and guide AI use cases

Microsoft 365	AI Services
Understand the M365 ecosystem	Understand the AI ecosystem (Copilot, ChatGPT, Gemini, etc.)
Offer ongoing support and QBRs	Offer ongoing usage monitoring, guidance, and updates

You don't need to build automations or train AI models.

Just like you don't write Excel formulas for clients... you don't need to engineer AI agents either.

You curate, advise, provision, train, and support. That's your role.

Provision. Secure. Train. Support.

Here's how it looks in practice with AI:

1. **Help clients choose the right tools**

   Maybe it's Microsoft Copilot. Maybe it's ChatGPT Team. Maybe it's Perplexity Pro for research or Synthesia for video. You're not picking the "best AI"— you're matching tools to needs. And remember, a client may need multiple AI tools depending on their needs.

2. **Set up secure environments**

   Just like you configure M365 with MFA and compliance settings, you'll set policies for AI use. Setup SSO. Help answer: Which tools are allowed? What data can be used? What should never be entered into prompts?

3. **Train their employees**

   Like with Outlook or Teams, most employees are on their own unless you train them. Show them how to use AI responsibly. Teach them how to prompt. Share examples that make sense for their job.

4. **Support and monitor usage**

   Just like you monitor backups or email logs, you'll help clients understand AI usage. Are tools being used? Are there risks? Are some departments flying ahead while others lag behind?

You've Already Built This Muscle

You didn't become a certified Microsoft Office Specialist: Excel Expert to sell Microsoft 365. You became a trusted advisor. You knew how to align the right licenses, policies, and security—and then you gave clients the tools to be productive.

Now you'll do the same with AI. And just like Microsoft 365 created a whole services economy for MSPs... *AI will too.*

Don't Sell Expertise. Sell Enablement.

Remember this:

You're not paid to be the smartest person in the room. You're paid to be the one who makes it work... who makes it safe... who makes it scalable... and who makes it make sense.

That's the opportunity here. You already have the model. Now, just apply it to the next wave.

The Bottom Line

If you can support Microsoft 365, you can support AI.

It's the same motion:

- Choose the right tool
- Set up the environment
- Train the employees
- Monitor usage
- Provide ongoing support

- Deliver ROI

You don't need to be a data scientist. You just need to do what you already do best:

Enable clients to succeed with new technology—safely, productively, and with confidence.

Welcome to AI. You're more ready than you think.

4

YOUR CLIENTS ARE

ALREADY USING AI (POORLY)

Want to know the biggest misconception MSPs have about AI?

"My clients aren't using it yet."

Wrong.

Your clients are using AI. They just haven't told you.

Why? Because they didn't ask for permission. They didn't need a license from you. They didn't have to go through procurement. They opened a browser, went to ChatGPT, and started typing.

And now they're pasting client data into public models, using free-tier tools with zero security controls, and trusting AI outputs that may be flat-out wrong.

Welcome to Shadow AI.

Shadow AI Is the New Shadow IT

Remember when cloud storage tools like Dropbox started popping up inside client networks without IT's knowledge?

Sales reps used it to send proposals.

Marketing uploaded media kits.

HR stored onboarding docs.

None of it was vetted. None of it was secure.

But it was easy, fast, and worked better than whatever "official" solution was in place.

AI is following the exact same pattern. And once again, IT has been left out of the loop.

The Real Risks of Shadow AI

Let's be clear: AI tools themselves aren't dangerous. The danger is in how untrained users interact with them.

Here's what's happening in your clients' environments right now—and the specific risks each scenario creates:

1. Sensitive Data Exposure

- **A salesperson copies an entire prospect database**—names, company details, revenue figures—into ChatGPT to personalize 50 outreach emails at once, not realizing that data now lives in OpenAI's systems forever.

- **An accountant feeds three years of financial statements into ChatGPT** to "help analyze trends," inadvertently giving AI access to cash flow, profit margins, and strategic financial data that competitors would pay millions to see.

- **An HR director uploads the entire employee handbook, salary data, and performance reviews** to "test" a new AI tool they saw recommended on LinkedIn, not knowing if that data gets stored, shared, or used for training.

2. Shadow Tools and Extensions

- **A support rep installs a "helpful" AI browser extension** that automatically reads every support ticket, customer email, and internal chat—sending your most sensitive customer communications to an unvetted third-party server.

3. Trusting AI Without Validation

- **A marketer asks Claude to write a blog post about your biggest competitor**, then publishes completely fabricated "market research" and false claims that could trigger a defamation lawsuit.

- **Finance makes budget decisions based on AI analysis** that used flawed assumptions about market trends.

- **Customer service sends AI-written responses** that contain incorrect product information, leading to angry customers and returned orders.

4. Compliance Violations

- **A medical assistant uses ChatGPT to help write patient follow-up emails**, copying and pasting patient names, conditions, and treatment details— turning every interaction into a potential HIPAA violation.

- **A paralegal uploads case files and client communications to Claude** for "research assistance," potentially destroying attorney-client privilege and exposing litigation strategy to opposing counsel.

5. Security Blind Spots

AI doesn't trip alerts in your MDR. Your SIEM won't catch an employee using an AI app, especially on their phone. And none of your security tools will stop a data leak if it happens in a prompt box.

Here's why traditional security tools can't help:

- Your firewalls can't see what employees type into web forms.

- Your DLP tools don't monitor browser-based AI conversations.

- Your security awareness training doesn't cover AI-specific risks.

- Your backup systems can't restore data that's been fed into AI training models.

Traditional security tools weren't built for this. None of this is malicious. But it's all untrained, unmanaged, and invisible.

That's the danger.

What's Driving the Problem?

Simple: curiosity + lack of training.

People want to try these tools. They've heard about them. Their peers are using them. Friends and family are using them. They've seen the TikToks and LinkedIn posts.

But no one has told them what's safe to use or what data is off-limits. No one explained how to verify outputs or which tools are actually approved for business use.

No one taught them how to ask good prompts or what the real risks are. They're experimenting blindly because nobody gave them a roadmap.

So they move fast, alone, and in the dark.

That's the opportunity.

How Widespread Is This?

This isn't happening to "other" companies. It's happening everywhere.

Recent research[1] reveals the shocking scope of Shadow AI adoption:

- **42% of office workers** are using generative AI tools like ChatGPT at work

- **1 in 3 of those workers** (roughly 14% of all employees) say they keep their AI use secret from their employers

- **65% of employees using ChatGPT** rely on the free tier, where their company data can be used to train AI models

- **20% of employees** report secretly using AI during job interviews

- A McKinsey report found that **employees are using AI for significantly more of their work than their leaders think they are**

- These aren't just tech companies or early adopters—this is happening across every industry, at every company size.

The most concerning finding: Most of this usage is happening in the shadows because employees fear being judged as incompetent or replaceable.

---

[1] Axios – "Secret chatbot use causes workplace rifts," May 29, 2025. https://www.axios.com/2025/05/29/secret-chatgpt-workplace

What this means for MSPs

If these statistics hold true, then roughly **1 in 7 employees at every client** is secretly using AI tools—often the free versions that offer zero data protection.

And that's just the ones willing to admit it in a survey.

The reality: Every single one of your clients has employees using ungoverned AI tools right now. The only question is whether you'll help them manage the risk before something goes wrong.

The window for proactive intervention is closing fast. Once a data breach or compliance violation happens, you're managing damage instead of preventing it.

The Moment to Lead Is Now

You don't need to block AI tools. You don't need to stop employees from experimenting. But you do need to help your clients build awareness about what their teams are already doing and what the real risks are.

Help them define policies that encourage safe experimentation instead of driving usage underground.

Train employees so they know which tools are approved, what data is off-limits, and how to verify AI outputs before acting on them.

Deploy safe, secure tools with proper licensing and oversight instead of letting teams use whatever free version they find online.

Monitor usage so you can spot problems early and celebrate wins.

Turn AI into an advantage that makes them more competitive, not a liability that creates risk.

That's how you lead.

Just like we did with cybersecurity. We didn't stop people from clicking links. We trained them to spot the dangerous ones.

Now, it's the same with AI.

Your Message to Clients

Here's what you should be telling your clients, right now:

"Your employees are already using AI tools. And if they're untrained, they could be exposing your business to serious risk.

The answer isn't to ban AI—it's to train for it. We can help you do that."

That message is powerful. It's real and it resonates. Because once you open their eyes to what's already happening, they'll see why they need you.

The Bottom Line

Shadow AI isn't coming—it's already here.

Right now, 1 in 7 employees at every client is secretly using AI tools without policies, training, or oversight.

They're uploading sensitive data, trusting unverified outputs, and creating compliance risks that traditional security tools can't detect.

This isn't a future problem you can plan for. It's a current reality you need to address.

The choice is simple: Lead the conversation now, or manage the crisis later.

Start with one conversation:

"Your employees are already using AI. Let's make sure they're doing it safely."

That's your opening. That's your opportunity. That's how you become the trusted guide through their next transformation.

Now that you understand the risks your clients face, let's talk about how to have these conversations in a way that leads to action, not paralysis.

5

MAKING AI RELATABLE:

THE INTERN MINDSET THAT SELLS

Want a simple, powerful way to explain AI to a client? Tell them this:

"Think of AI like an intern. A really smart, really fast, but occasionally wrong intern."

This metaphor works... because it reframes AI from something abstract and intimidating... to something human, familiar, and manageable.

It lowers the temperature of the conversation.

It makes the risks relatable.

And it sets the right expectations for both value and oversight.

It's Not the Tools!

The uncomfortable truth is that most SMBs don't care about ChatGPT, Claude, or Copilot. They care about invoices getting out faster, customer emails getting answered on time, and they care about sales and closing more deals.

Fewer mistakes. More capacity. More control.

They care about business outcomes.

This chapter shows you how to bridge that gap—using the intern mindset to make AI both understandable and irresistible to SMB clients.

Why the Intern Analogy Works

Think about how a real intern operates.

They can help with research, writing, and tasks. They're eager and capable, but they need direction.

They need guidance, clear instructions, and supervision because, if left alone, they'll go down rabbit holes or miss the point entirely.

They can be a huge help, but only if you train them well and set clear expectations.

They make mistakes, sometimes obvious ones, but they learn quickly from feedback.

Most importantly, they don't replace your team. They enhance it by taking on the work that frees up your experts to do expert-level thinking.

Now think about how AI tools like ChatGPT, Copilot, and Perplexity behave. Sound familiar? It's the same dynamic.

And when you help your clients see AI this way, something clicks.

"Oh. This isn't magic. But it's useful. And I need to manage it."

That's the goal. But here's where most MSPs get it wrong...

They lead with the tools instead of the outcomes.

The Fatal Mistake: Leading with Features

Instead of saying:

> *"You should check out Copilot for Word. It's amazing."*

Say:

> "We can help your team write proposals 40% faster."

Instead of:

> *"ChatGPT has new memory capabilities."*

Try:

> "You can get a weekly summary of your meetings and to-dos—with action items ready to go."

Tools are impressive.

Tasks are relatable.

Speak in Use Cases, Not Features

Let's look at a few side-by-side comparisons.

AI Feature Hype	SMB Relatable Use Case
"Natural language data querying"	"Your finance manager can ask plain-English questions about revenue trends."
"Generative AI content creation"	"Your marketing coordinator can write a month of blog content in a day."
"Automated summarization"	"You can instantly get bullet points from your sales calls without writing notes."
"AI assistants for research"	"Your team can find competitor pricing or market stats in five minutes."
"Prompt engineering"	"We'll give your team examples of what to type to get great results."

Use their language. Not ours.

How to Use the Intern Mindset With Clients

Here's how to position the concept:

- "Think of ChatGPT as an intern who has read everything on the internet."
- "Your intern is fast—but they're not always accurate."
- "You need to teach your intern how to help you. And double-check their work."
- "The better your instructions, the better the results."
- "You wouldn't give an intern a confidential file without training them. The same goes for AI."

This removes fear and overhype at the same time. It makes AI accessible without being dangerous.

What the Intern Can Do

(That You Couldn't Afford Before)

AI interns aren't just faster, they're capable of things most SMBs have never had access to.

For a dentist:

- Can I use AI to write post-visit instructions for each patient?
- Can it help us write responses to Google reviews?
- Can it create email follow-ups for patients with overdue appointments?

For a law firm:

- Summarize case law research
- Draft contract templates
- Create client communication templates

For any SMB:

- Every employee now has a personal researcher
- A marketer can generate five ad headlines in seconds

- A support team can summarize long tickets automatically
- A sales rep can prep for calls with deep prospect insight
- Legal can write contracts or policies with guidance
- Finance can do a SWOT analysis on a proposed price increase

Before AI, SMBs couldn't afford these capabilities. Now, they can. That's the power of the intern mindset. It's not just about saving time—it's about unlocking new abilities.

Training the Intern: The Power of Prompting

The secret to a great AI intern? Training it with better prompts.

Prompting is how you:

- Set the intern's role
- Define the task
- Give it examples
- Guide tone, format, and outcome
- Clarify the audience
- Establish review checkpoints

And just like with a real intern, if you give vague instructions, you get vague results. This is why prompting is the core skill every employee needs.

It's not about learning a new language. It's about being a better delegator.

Examples of Training Your AI Intern

Just like training a real intern, the quality of your instructions determines the quality of the results.

Poor Instructions:

- "Write an email"

- "Help with marketing"
- "Analyze this data"
- "Create a proposal"

Better Instructions:

- "Write a professional follow-up email to a client who missed their appointment, offering to reschedule and expressing understanding. Keep it under 100 words and include our scheduling link."

- "Create 3 LinkedIn posts promoting our new cybersecurity service. Each should be under 280 characters, use a confident but helpful tone, and include a call-to-action."

- "Review this quarterly sales data and identify the top 3 trends I should discuss with my team. Include specific numbers and actionable recommendations for each trend."

- "Draft a 2-page proposal for IT support services for a 25-person law firm. Include our standard service tiers, response times, and emphasize our legal industry experience."

The difference? Specific role, clear task, defined format, target audience, and success criteria.

Supervising the Intern: Avoiding AI Mistakes

Even a well-trained intern needs oversight.

Your clients must understand:

- AI makes stuff up.
- AI has no judgment.
- AI doesn't know your business.
- AI will confidently get it wrong.

That's why review and human judgment are essential.

Teach your clients to:

- Always fact-check external outputs
- Never paste in sensitive data
- Treat AI as a first draft, not a final product
- Use AI to accelerate, not automate blindly

The intern is a helper—not a replacement for thought, ethics, or responsibility.

Tell Better Stories That Sell

Facts tell. Stories sell.

Start collecting real client wins (or your own internal use cases).

Keep them short. Specific. Measurable.

Examples:

- "One of our clients cut employee onboarding time by 30% using AI to generate training docs."

- "A client in real estate now creates listing descriptions in half the time with better SEO."

- "Our own SDR team uses Perplexity to research prospects—5 minutes of prep instead of 30."

These stories make AI feel real. They create "aha" moments.

Industry-Specific Intern Examples

Don't just say "AI." Say how AI helps their business.

Healthcare Practice: "Your AI intern can draft patient follow-up emails, create treatment plan summaries, and help write responses to online reviews—all while keeping patient data secure."

Manufacturing Company: "Think of AI as an intern who can help write safety procedures, create training materials, and draft vendor communications faster than any human assistant."

Professional Services: "Your AI intern can research prospects, draft proposals, summarize client meetings, and create project status reports—giving you back hours each week."

Accounting Firms: "Generate tax planning narratives, create audit documentation, draft client advisories."

Real Estate: "Write property descriptions, create market analysis summaries, draft client communications."

Architecture Firms: "Draft project proposals, create client presentation materials, summarize building code requirements."

Insurance Agencies: "Create policy summaries, draft claim explanations, write renewal letters."

The more specific, the more it resonates.

Real ROI > Cool Tools

Every SMB is asking:

"If I spend money on this, will it actually help?"

That's your golden moment. Because with AI, ROI is fast.

- A $30/month Copilot license? Paid for in the first 30 minutes of time saved.

- One AI-generated sales email that lands a deal? The tool paid for itself for a year.

- Five hours/month saved across 10 employees at $25/hour = $15,000/year in reclaimed productivity. Real money.

Translate tools into time, money, and growth. That's how you win the conversation.

The Right Message Framework

Here's what to say:

- "This isn't an experiment. It's a productivity upgrade."

- "AI isn't just for tech companies. It's for every team that uses email, documents, or data."

- "Your competitors are already experimenting. Let's make sure you're doing it safely—and better."

- "We'll help your employees become more effective, not just faster."

Handling Different Client Types

The Skeptic

What they say: "I'm not sure about this AI stuff—it feels like hype to me."

Your response: "That's exactly why we start small. Let's pick one simple task and show you what's possible."

The Overwhelmed Owner

What they say: "This all sounds complicated. I don't have time to learn another technology."

Your response: "You don't need to learn AI. You just need someone you trust to guide you through it. That's what we're here for."

The Early Adopter

What they say: "I've been reading about AI and I'm excited to try it!"

Your response: "I love that you're already thinking about this. Let's make sure you're doing it safely and getting the most value."

The Penny Pincher

What they say: "These AI tools seem expensive for what they do."

Your response: "The cost of not adopting AI is higher than the cost of adopting it badly. We'll help you do it right from the start."

From Intern to Impact

The intern mindset creates the right culture.

One where employees feel safe to experiment without fear of making mistakes or being judged.

Where they're encouraged to share wins and discoveries with their teammates instead of hoarding knowledge.

Where they understand what's at stake—both the opportunities and the risks—so they make smart decisions about when and how to use AI.

Where they see AI as a tool that makes them more capable, not a threat that might replace them.

Where they become smarter problem-solvers, not just faster task-completers.

That's when the real value shows up. Because once your clients start treating AI like an intern—training it, guiding it, managing it—it becomes a force multiplier for productivity.

And that's where MSPs can shine.

By helping clients:

- Set policies
- Provide training
- Select the right tools
- Manage risk
- Measure success

You become the bridge from AI hype to AI impact.

The Bottom Line

Don't sell AI tools. Start selling productivity.

The intern analogy works because it's relatable, manageable, and sets the right expectations. Clients don't care about ChatGPT's latest features—they care about getting invoices out faster and closing more deals.

Your job isn't to impress them with technology.

Your job is to show them how AI solves real problems.

Lead with outcomes, not features. Speak their language, not yours. Share stories, not statistics.

When clients see AI as a helpful intern that needs training and supervision—not magic or a threat—they'll understand why they need you to guide the process.

That's how you turn AI curiosity into AI revenue.

6

TRAINING IS YOUR TROJAN HORSE:

THE STRATEGIC PATH TO AI LEADERSHIP

Here's the biggest lie in AI adoption:

"Just give employees access—they'll figure it out."

No, they won't.

Not well. Not safely and not consistently.

We've seen this movie before... with Microsoft 365... with cybersecurity... with the cloud.

And every time, the lesson is the same:

Without training, tools don't get used—or worse, get used dangerously.

Here's what most MSPs don't realize. AI training isn't just about education. It's your Trojan Horse.

Just like Security Awareness Training (SAT) helped MSPs break into cybersecurity, AI Awareness Training is your foot in the door for the entire AI adoption journey.

Why Training Is Your Modern-Day Trojan Horse

How did MSPs start talking to clients about cybersecurity? It didn't start with SOCs or MDRs or compliance frameworks. It started with something every client understood:

"Your employees are the weakest link."

SAT gave MSPs a way to introduce cybersecurity without needing to be security experts. It was simple, valuable, and easy to explain.

Fast-forward to today, because AI Awareness Training is your modern-day Trojan Horse. It's the easiest, fastest way to help clients adopt AI—and to position your MSP as their trusted advisor.

What makes it a Trojan Horse?

- It's the low-risk, high-reward offer that leads to bigger conversations.
- It's the service your client says yes to—even if they're not ready to "go all in" on AI yet.
- It's how you build trust before talking strategy, integration, or roadmaps.

Training makes AI real. It surfaces risks. It generates momentum. And it opens the door to everything that comes next.

Why Training Is Essential

(And Why Tools Alone Aren't Enough)

Yes, ChatGPT is easy to open and type into. But that's not the same as using it effectively or safely.

The myth of "intuitive" tools has hurt businesses before. Just because employees can access AI doesn't mean they understand:

- How to write effective prompts
- How to verify AI outputs
- What data is safe to input
- Which tools are approved for business use
- Where AI adds the most value in their specific role

When employees aren't trained, they either underuse the tools, misuse them dangerously, or avoid them altogether.

That's exactly why training works so well as your entry point:

1. Every Client Needs It

Their employees are already using AI tools—with or without permission. That means they already have risk, but no policy and no plan.

2. The Threat is Already Here

Cybercriminals are already leveraging AI. More sophisticated phishing emails. Deepfake scams. Social engineering attacks.

Even if your clients aren't ready to adopt AI internally, they're already being targeted by AI-powered threats. Training helps them recognize and defend against these evolving risks.

3. It Doesn't Require Deep Technical Expertise

You don't need to build custom agents. You just need to teach fundamentals: safe usage, effective prompting, and business applications.

4. It Creates Immediate, Visible Value

Clients see employees using tools more effectively, with less fear and fewer mistakes.

5. It Positions You as the AI Leader

When you deliver training, clients naturally look to you for tool recommendations, policy decisions, and strategic guidance.

What AI Awareness Training Should Cover

If you're building AI training for your clients, keep it simple and focused. Your goal isn't to turn employees into prompt engineers, it's to help them understand the tools, use them safely, and get real work done.

Here's what strong AI training should include:

1. Demystify the Tool

- What is generative AI (in plain English)?
- How do tools like ChatGPT, Copilot, and Perplexity actually work?
- How is AI different from search engines or scripts?
- Remove the fear. Build confidence.

2. Teach Prompting Basics

- The core pattern:
  Context → Instruction → Output Format
- How to iterate and refine prompts
- Practical examples by role (sales, marketing, HR, support)

3. Establish Guardrails

- What's safe to input—and what's not
- Risks of hallucinations, bias, and misinformation
- Why human review still matters

4. Connect AI to the Job

1. "Before and after" use cases by department
2. Quick wins: tasks AI can make faster, better, or easier
3. Role-specific examples employees can try right away

5. Normalize the Conversation

- Encourage open use, not quiet experimenting
- Share wins across the team
- Position AI as a tool, not a threat

6. AI Cybersecurity Training

- How to spot AI-generated phishing emails
- Recognizing deepfake audio and video scams
- Understanding AI-powered social engineering tactics
- Red flags in AI-generated content
- When to verify information that seems "too perfect"

If your training checks those six boxes, you're 80% of the way there.

Now layer in resources to keep it going:

Bonus Resources That Make Training Stick

Acceptable Use Policy: Set expectations early

Prompt Library PDF: Prebuilt examples by role

Weekly AI Tips Newsletter: Keep it fresh and ongoing

Training doesn't need to be complex. It needs to be clear, safe, and job-relevant.

Scaling Training Through Platform Partners

You may be thinking "I don't have the resources to provide training to every employee at every client."

You're right. Training doesn't scale very well when delivered one-on-one. But just like with Security Awareness Training, specialized platforms have emerged to help MSPs scale training delivery to their clients.

Companies like Breach Secure Now (BSN), KnowBe4, and other training providers have built platforms specifically designed for MSP partners to resell and scale awareness training programs.

Benefits of Partnering with a Training Platform

You get professionally developed curriculum that is continuously updated as AI tools evolve and new risks emerge.

Automated delivery and tracking systems handle the heavy lifting of scheduling, reminders, and progress monitoring.

White-label or co-branded options let you maintain your brand relationship with clients.

Scalable pricing models are designed for MSP resale, so you can mark up services appropriately.

Partnering reduces your development time and ongoing maintenance. You focus on client relationships while the platform handles content creation and updates.

What to Look for in a Training Partner

Find providers with MSP-friendly pricing and support that understand your business model and client needs.

Look for industry-specific content customization so you can serve healthcare, legal, manufacturing, and other verticals effectively.

Integration with your existing client management systems makes deployment and tracking seamless.

Regular content updates as AI tools evolve keep training relevant and current.

Comprehensive reporting and analytics give you the data to prove ROI and track adoption across your client base.

This approach lets you realize the benefits of providing comprehensive training without having to build a training platform from scratch.

Whether you build your own training program or partner with an existing platform, the key is getting started and positioning yourself as the AI education leader for your clients.

How Training Opens Every Door

Training isn't the end goal—it's the strategic beginning.

Here's what happens after you deliver training:

Immediate Results (0-30 days)

Employees start using AI tools more confidently.

Questions and requests for guidance increase.

Department heads notice productivity improvements.

Natural Expansion (30-90 days)

Clients ask for tool recommendations and provisioning.

Requests for department-specific use case development.

Need for usage monitoring and reporting emerges.

Strategic Services Needed (90+ days)

- Refining AI policy creation and governance
- Prompt library development
- Ongoing enablement and coaching
- vAIO (Virtual AI Officer) strategic services

The progression is natural and client-driven. You're not pushing services—you're responding to needs that surface naturally because of training.

Training gives you a seat at the strategy table. Everything else flows from that trusted advisory position.

Marketing Your Training Services

Here are six tactics that work:

1. AI Readiness Assessment

This shows how a client can benefit from AI adoption. It looks at various departments and shows AI use cases. This opens up the AI conversation with clients. Offer it as a free or paid diagnostic.

2. Live Webinars or Lunch-and-Learns

"AI for [Industry]" or "The Truth About AI Risk"

3. Client Stories

Share before/after productivity wins.

4. AI Use Case Library

Publish a PDF of how real SMBs are using AI.

5. Weekly AI Tip Email

Build authority and trust over time.

6. Onboarding Bundles

Include AI training in new client onboarding.

The best part? You can start now. You don't need a full LMS or 10-part course to begin.

Start with:

- A one-hour workshop
- A short recorded training
- A team lunch-and-learn
- A prompt cheat sheet by department
- A PDF with dos and don'ts for AI usage

Or partner with an AI Awareness Training company. Then evolve.

The Trojan Horse That Builds an Empire

AI Awareness Training is relatable, low-cost, low-complexity, immediately valuable, easy to package, and widely needed.

Best of all?

It positions your MSP for everything that comes next: strategic services where you guide long-term AI adoption plans, automation consulting where you help streamline repetitive business processes, workflow integration where you connect AI tools with existing systems, and full-scale AI enablement where you become their trusted partner for ongoing growth.

Start with training. Then go wherever the client needs to go next. You'll already be leading the way.

The Bottom Line

Training is your foot in the door. Just like Security Awareness Training was your entry point into cybersecurity, AI Awareness Training is your entry point into AI.

But AI is moving faster than cybersecurity ever did. The window is now. Start with training. Win the relationship. Build the future.

Make AI as familiar as hiring an intern—and as valuable as hiring ten. That's the roadmap.

7

The AI Consultant Threat

(And Why MSPs Must Lead)

Let's rewind the clock to 2010.

If you were supporting healthcare clients back then, you probably remember a massive change sweeping the industry: Meaningful Use.

Billions in government incentives were pushing medical practices to adopt electronic health records (EHR). And for MSPs like mine, it was a gold rush. We were wiring offices, installing servers, securing networks.

But there was a problem.

EHR consultants showed up.

These consultants weren't IT people. They weren't interested in your managed services. But they had the ear of the client—and they were suddenly telling MSPs how to set up the network, what kind of performance was required, and which hardware to buy.

Medical practices and hospitals brought in these consultants. They knew clinical workflows. They knew the different EHRs and which one would be best for the medical practice. They gave advice that we couldn't give.

They were the strategic voice in the room. We were just the tech implementers.

They became the ones clients trusted to "lead" technology decisions.

Sound familiar? It should—because AI is replaying that same dynamic. And if MSPs don't lead their clients into AI adoption, AI consultants will.

The Rise of the AI Consultant

Right now, there are consultants popping up everywhere who know how to build GPT agents, have experience creating automations and workflows, know how to navigate business operations and change management, and are positioning themselves as the experts on AI strategy.

They're showing up in legal, healthcare, marketing, real estate, manufacturing... and they're knocking on your clients' doors.

> *"We'll help you build your AI roadmap."*

> *"We'll train your staff."*

> *"We'll set up automation to make your business more efficient."*

They're not trying to replace your help desk.

They don't want to sell firewalls.

But they will get between you and your client's most strategic decisions.

That's the threat.

Warning Signs: How to Spot Consultant Activity

Your client may be talking to AI consultants when they start asking:

> *"Can you help us develop an AI roadmap?"*

> *"We need a digital transformation strategy."*

"Someone wants to do a workflow analysis of our business processes."

"We're looking at automation opportunities across departments."

"Do you know about AI governance frameworks?"

"We need help with change management for new technology."

Other red flags

- New terminology around "AI strategy" or "digital optimization"

- Requests for detailed process documentation

- Questions about integrating AI with existing systems

- Mentions of "efficiency studies" or "productivity assessments"

- Leadership asking about AI ROI measurement

When you hear these signals, you may be playing defense and not offense.

And this time... they're not going away

Unlike the EHR consultants who came, implemented, and left... AI consultants aren't just there for a deployment. They're there for the long haul, because AI is evolving rapidly.

Workflows will need constant iteration as teams discover what works and what doesn't. Prompts and use cases will be continually optimized as employees get better at directing AI tools. Security and compliance concerns will shift as regulations catch up to the technology. New tools will be evaluated every quarter as the market explodes with options.

This isn't a one-time project. It's an ongoing transformation... from department to department... from employee to employee, automating workflow after workflow.

And that means whoever leads AI adoption will become the ongoing strategic advisor.

The Competitor in Sheep's Clothing

Right now your competition is other MSPs. But with AI, your competitors are AI consultants. These consultants are telling your clients they can work side by side with your MSP.

That is the danger. Your client doesn't need to replace you.

They can bring in someone more strategic. That could be the same or worse than being replaced.

Why You Can't Afford to Sit This Out

Here is an uncomfortable truth: some MSPs are waiting.

They're saying:

> *"We're focused on cybersecurity right now."*
>
> *"Clients aren't asking for AI help."*
>
> *"There's no way to monetize this yet."*

All understandable. But dangerous. Because while you wait for demand to show up on your doorstep, someone else is building relationships with your clients.

Someone else is learning their workflows.

Someone else is sitting in on leadership meetings.

Someone else is advising on data strategy, automation, compliance.

The good news is that your clients trust you. You have the relationship. They don't want to bring in another vendor. They don't want an AI consultant. But you need to lead the conversation and start them on their journey.

Give them a reason to say to a consultant:

"Thanks, but my MSP is handling this."

How to Lead Before You're Asked

Here's what worked in cybersecurity—and will work again with AI:

The Immediate Action Plan (This Week)

1. **Start using AI tools internally and document specific wins.**

   - Use ChatGPT for client communication drafts
   - Try Copilot for meeting summaries and follow-ups
   - Test Perplexity for client research and preparation
   - More detail on internal adoption is found in Chapter 10 (Internal First)

2. **Identify your 3 most vulnerable clients**

   - High-growth companies looking for competitive advantage
   - Businesses with repetitive, manual processes
   - Organizations that have adopted new technology quickly in the past

3. **Schedule "AI Risk Assessment" conversations**

   - Position as cybersecurity extension: "Part of our security review"
   - Use the shadow AI statistics from Chapter 4
   - Offer to help them understand what employees are already doing

The 30-Day Plan

1. **Deliver AI awareness training to your top 5 clients**
   - Start with a free or paid AI readiness assessment
   - Position as risk mitigation, not technology sales
   - Focus on employee safety and productivity

2. **Create AI policy templates for your key industries**
   - Customize acceptable use policies by vertical
   - Include data classification guidelines

3. **Begin quarterly AI discussions in your QBRs**
   - "What's your current AI strategy?"
   - "Are employees using AI tools safely?"
   - "How can we help you stay ahead of competitors?"

The 90-Day Goal

Be positioned as the trusted AI advisor before consultants arrive.

Competitive Positioning

(What to Say When Consultants Show Up)

When clients say:

"We're working with an AI consultant..."

You say:

"That's great! We love supporting AI implementations. We handle the technical foundation—security, integration, compliance—while they focus on strategy. Most AI projects fail because the technical foundation isn't solid."

Then pivot to:

"Have they addressed data security and employee training yet? That's where we see most AI projects get stuck. We can make sure their recommendations are implemented safely."

When clients ask:

"Do we need an AI consultant?"

You say:

"It depends on your goals. If you want to optimize complex workflows across multiple departments, a consultant might help. But if you want to help employees be more productive safely, we can handle that with training and policies. Most businesses should start with the foundation before building the fancy stuff."

When consultants position against you:

"IT departments slow down AI adoption..."

Your response:

"Security and compliance aren't obstacles—they're what allow businesses to scale AI confidently. We help you move fast *and* safely. The last thing you want is a data breach because someone bypassed IT protocols."

The Partnership Strategy

Sometimes working *with* consultants is the right move.

When to partner

- Client needs complex workflow redesign beyond your expertise

- Large organization requiring change management specialists
- Industry-specific AI applications you don't understand

How to maintain control

- Position yourself as the technical foundation partner
- Own the security, compliance, and integration workstreams
- Maintain the ongoing support relationship
- Ensure consultants understand your role in implementation

Remember the key principle: You can collaborate without surrendering your strategic position.

AI Should Be Part of Your MSP Identity

Here's the truth:

You're already selling productivity (M365, Google Workspace). You're already selling risk management (cybersecurity). You're already enabling business outcomes. AI is just the next layer on top of all of that.

You don't need to pivot away from your core. You just need to integrate AI into the services and conversations you're already having.

Positioning Yourself as the AI Guide

You *don't* need to build agents from scratch or customize APIs for complex integrations. You *don't* need to compete with OpenAI or Microsoft on developing better models. You *don't* need to know everything about every AI tool that launches each week.

You *do* need to use AI yourself so you can speak from experience, not theory. Educate your clients about opportunities and risks so they make informed decisions. Help them adopt safely with proper policies and training. Keep up with AI products and innovations enough to guide tool selection. Deliver consistent value through practical guidance and support.

When you do these things consistently, you'll earn a seat at the AI strategy table by proving you understand their business needs.

That's enough.

Your Window Is Closing

Market timeline:

- **Today**

  Most SMBs have no AI strategy

- **6 months**

  AI consultants will be established in major markets

- **12 months**

  Clients will expect their MSP to have AI expertise

- **18 months**

  Late MSPs will struggle to compete

The choice is yours. You can lead now while the field is open and you can build relationships without heavy competition. Or you can follow later when it's crowded and you're fighting for scraps against established AI consultants.

Or even worse? You'll get left behind completely while your clients get their strategic guidance from someone else.

The Bottom Line

You have a choice to make: Wait for clients to ask for AI help, or lead them there. The MSPs who lead will own the AI conversation. The ones who wait will implement someone else's strategy.

Start this week. Your clients need you to guide them through this, just like you did with cybersecurity and the cloud. This time, the opportunity is bigger. And the window won't stay open forever.

I recommend you lead consistently—with training, policies, and practical guidance. This way, the consultants won't take your seat.

You'll already be sitting in it.

8

FROM EXPERIMENTS TO INFRASTRUCTURE:

THE STRATEGIC CONVERSATION PLAYBOOK

The AI intern analogy is a great place to start, but it's not where the journey ends. Over time, your clients will move from seeing AI as a novelty or experiment, to seeing it as infrastructure, just like email, file storage, security tools, and line-of-business apps became expected parts of doing business.

AI will become embedded into daily operations, expected in every department, and necessary for staying competitive.

The challenge? Most MSPs struggle with how to talk about this transformation. They either avoid the topic entirely, or talk about it in ways that confuse, overwhelm, or alienate their clients. Meanwhile, AI consultants are booking meetings and building relationships.

This chapter shows you how to guide clients through the mindset shift from experimentation to integration—and how to have AI conversations that actually land and lead to business.

The Evolution Most Companies Go Through

Here's the journey your clients will take:

1. **Curiosity**: "We're hearing about this ChatGPT thing— what can it do?"

2. **Experimentation**: "Let's try it for sales emails or blog posts."

3. **Adoption**: "Some teams are using it regularly. It's actually helping."

4. **Integration**: "Let's connect it to our CRM or SOPs."

5. **Infrastructure**: "We expect every employee to use AI to be more effective."

Your job as an MSP is to guide this journey—and to anticipate what clients will need at each phase.

But here's the key: *You can't wait for them to ask.*

You need to start these conversations proactively, before AI consultants do.

What *Not* to Do in AI Conversations

Let's start with the traps to avoid:

Don't Lead with Tools

Saying "You should use ChatGPT" is like saying "You should use a spreadsheet" without explaining why or how.

Don't Talk Like a Futurist

Terms like "AGI," "multi-modal," or "agents" don't land with SMBs. They create distance, not clarity.

Don't Focus on Fear or FOMO

Leading with "You're going to be left behind!" rarely inspires action. It often causes paralysis.

Don't Assume They Care Yet

Just because AI is exciting to you doesn't mean it's a priority for your client. Make it relevant.

Don't Wait for Perfect Timing

There's no perfect moment. The best time to start AI conversations is during your existing touchpoints—QBRs, security reviews, strategy sessions.

What to Do Instead

Start smart.

Lead with Security and Risk

Your strongest opening? Position AI as a security and governance issue:

> "As part of our security review, we need to talk about AI usage. We're seeing companies get hit with data breaches because employees are using AI tools without proper policies."

This works because it's a natural extension of your existing role as their trusted security advisor. Clients already trust you with security decisions, so AI governance feels like the logical next step. It creates urgency without being pushy. You're highlighting a real risk they may not have considered.

You're solving a problem, not selling a product. You're protecting them from something that's already happening. As we learned in Chapter 4, more than 40% of office workers are already using free generative AI tools like ChatGPT at work, and a third of those keep it a secret from their employers.

Without your guidance, these clients will remain unaware of the dangers until it's too late.

Use Their Language, Not Yours

Remember the intern analogy from Chapter 5? Apply that same principle to strategic conversations. Don't lead with technical features. Instead, lead with business outcomes they already understand:

Don't say: "We'll build you a GPT-powered automation assistant."

Say: "We'll help your team save hours by drafting follow-up emails and proposals faster."

Don't say: "We'll create AI-driven workflows that integrate with your CRM."

Say: "We'll help you automatically summarize client meetings and create next steps."

Translate AI into results they care about.

Bring Stories from Their Industry

In Chapter 5, I went into detail about telling relatable stories. When possible, use success stories that feel close to home.

"We helped a law firm use AI to summarize case law in seconds."

"A dental client now uses AI to draft responses to online reviews."

"A staffing firm reduced candidate screening time by 50% with AI summaries."

These stories spark ideas. They make AI feel real and achievable.

Position AI as a Business Tool, Not a Threat

Many business owners are secretly wondering:

"Will this replace my staff?"

"Is this safe?"

"Will it really help?"

Your job is to reassure, not hype:

> "This is like hiring an intern for every employee—for only $30 per month."

> "It's here to help your team, not replace them."

> "We'll show you how to use it safely, with policies and training."

A Natural Conversation Flow

Here's how to structure the conversation:

Opening (Connect to existing relationship)

> "You know how we help you stay secure with cybersecurity training? We're seeing the same need emerging with AI tools. Employees are using them, but without guidance."

Problem (Make it relevant)

> "A lot of SMBs are in the same boat—employees are starting to use tools like ChatGPT and Copilot, but no one's really managing it. That creates risk and missed opportunity."

Solution (Keep it simple)

> "We've developed a simple way to help companies like yours adopt AI safely. We start with employee training, help you put policies in place, and guide you through use cases that are already working for other businesses in your industry."

Next Step (Low pressure)

> "You don't need to go all-in, you just need to start. Want to chat more about it?"

Simple. Clear. Low-pressure.

Valuable.

Better Questions That Move Things Forward

Here are conversation starters that actually work:

- "Are any of your employees using ChatGPT or other AI tools right now?"

- "Would you like help making sure it's used securely and productively?"

- "Which departments would benefit from a digital assistant the most?"

- "What's taking up the most time in your day-to-day operations?"

- "Would it help if we ran a 30-minute workshop for your staff?"

These questions move you from "AI seller" to "AI partner."

Meeting Clients Where They Are

For the Curious (Stage 1)

Focus on risk mitigation and employee safety. Share the Shadow AI statistics from Chapter 4. Position as cybersecurity extension: "Let's make sure employees are using these tools safely."

For the Experimenters (Stage 2)

Deliver AI Awareness Training. Create Acceptable Use Policies. Help select appropriate tools for initial experiments. Monitor usage and gather success stories.

For the Early Adopters (Stage 3)

Expand to additional departments. Implement usage reporting. Develop department-specific prompt libraries. Begin strategic planning for broader adoption.

For the Integrators (Stage 4)

Design AI-enhanced workflows. Integrate tools with existing systems. Provide advanced training. Consider vAIO services.

For the Infrastructure-Minded (Stage 5)

Manage AI like any other technology stack. Provide ongoing optimization, strategic roadmap planning, competitive analysis, and benchmarking.

Handling the Consultant Threat

When clients mention AI consultants, say:

> "That's great that you're thinking strategically about AI. Most consultants focus on the business strategy side. We handle the technical foundation—security, integration, employee training—that makes their recommendations actually work. Should we coordinate?"

When you suspect consultant involvement, say:

> "Are you getting any outside advice on AI strategy? We want to make sure whatever direction you go, you have the technical infrastructure to support it safely."

Remember: You can collaborate without surrendering your strategic position.

Why the Infrastructure Mindset Matters

When AI becomes infrastructure, the conversation changes:

from "Can we use this?" *to* "How do we secure it?"

from "Is it helpful?" *to* "Is it standard?"

from "A few people use it" *to* "Everyone is expected to"

from "Let's try tools" *to* "Let's design systems"

And that shift opens the door for long-term MSP services like:

- Provisioning and access management
- Acceptable use policies and governance
- Role-based training and certification
- Prompt libraries and best practices
- Usage monitoring and optimization
- Strategic roadmapping and planning

You're no longer just helping clients test AI—you're helping them operationalize it. That's sticky. That's valuable. That's what MSPs are built to do.

Avoiding the "Tech Expert Trap"

As an MSP, you're used to being the technical expert. But with AI, your role is different. You're not there to dazzle with tools, you're there to guide with clarity. You don't need to know every feature of every AI product. You just need to help clients make sense of what matters.

Show them what's possible. Train their team. Build guardrails. Find high-impact wins. Be the steady voice in a noisy space.

That's how you earn trust.

Culture Before Code

You don't need APIs. You don't need agents. You don't need automation flows.

You need a culture of experimentation, education, visibility, safety, and encouragement. If you help your clients build that, everything else becomes easier.

It all starts with leadership buy-in, employee training, internal champions, and simple first wins.

The Goal Is Momentum, Not Mastery

You're not trying to turn your client into an AI-powered enterprise overnight. You're trying to help them feel confident, not confused, about what AI can and can't do for their business.

Help them start using AI safely with clear policies and approved tools instead of experimenting in the shadows. Build internal interest by showing early wins and encouraging employees to share their discoveries. Show them quick wins that prove value without requiring major process changes or big investments.

Get them asking "What else can we do?" instead of "Is this worth it?"

That's the journey. You don't need a perfect pitch. You need a simple, steady approach that builds trust over time.

Your Action Plan

This week

Start AI conversations during your existing client touchpoints. Use the security angle. Keep it simple.

This month

Have AI discussions with your top 10 clients. Track what resonates. Refine your approach.

This quarter

Position yourself as the AI advisor before consultants arrive. Convert conversations into training engagements and policy work.

The Bottom Line

Every client conversation is an opportunity to lead. Start with their problems. Show them possibilities. Guide them through the journey... from experiments to infrastructure... from curiosity to capability... from AI hype to AI impact.

The MSPs who start these conversations now will own the AI transformation. The ones who wait will be implementing someone else's strategy.

That's how you become indispensable.

9

Leading AI Adoption

One Department at a Time:

The Land-and-Expand Playbook

Here's a myth worth busting:

"To adopt AI, a business needs a company-wide rollout."

Nope.

In fact, the most successful AI adoption stories start small—in one department.

We know this works because we've done it ourselves. Chapter 11 will show exactly how we implemented this departmental approach at BSN, starting with our content team and expanding from there.

But here's what most MSPs don't realize: Departmental AI adoption isn't just good strategy—it's your competitive moat. While AI consultants are selling enterprise-wide transformations, you can deliver immediate wins that prove your value and lock in strategic relationships.

This chapter shows you exactly how to execute the land-and-expand strategy that keeps consultants out and keeps you in control.

Why Departmental Adoption Wins Every Time

Starting with one department does three critical things:

1. **Lowers the barrier to entry**: Smaller scope, faster decisions, lower risk

2. **Creates quick, visible wins**: Success stories sell themselves

3. **Spreads through peer momentum**: Internal champions become your sales force

But most importantly, it positions you as the strategic guide before consultants even get in the door. While they're scheduling discovery calls, you're delivering results.

Department Selection Strategy

Prioritize based on competitive advantage potential.

Tier 1: Start Here (Highest Success Probability)

Sales Teams

- **Strong:** Measurable outcomes (deals, response rates)
- **Strong:** Competitive pressure drives adoption
- **Strong:** Leadership visibility of results
- **Strong:** High communication volume = high AI value

Marketing Teams

- **Strong:** Content-heavy workflows perfect for AI
- **Strong:** Creative teams often early adopters
- **Strong:** Visible output that leadership notices
- **Strong:** Measurable engagement metrics

Tier 2: Strong Second Choice

HR Teams

- **Strong:** High-volume writing tasks

- **Strong:** Standardization needs that AI addresses
- **Strong:** Immediate efficiency gains
- **Caution:** May have compliance concerns

Support Teams

- **Strong:** Clear input/output workflows
- **Strong:** Customer satisfaction metrics
- **Strong:** High repetition volume
- **Caution:** Requires careful quality control

Tier 3: Build Trust First

Finance Teams

- **Caution:** Higher accuracy requirements
- **Caution:** More resistance to new tools
- **Caution:** Compliance and audit concerns
- **Strong:** High-value analytical insights when successful

The Four-Step Departmental Domination Framework

Step 1: Strategic Discovery (Week 1-2)

Don't just ask what's taking time. Ask strategic questions:

For Department Heads:

- "What processes do your competitors do faster than you?"
- "If you could eliminate 2 hours of daily admin work, what would your team focus on instead?"
- "Where do you see the biggest bottlenecks between good work and great work?"

- "What would help your department contribute more to company growth?"

For Leadership:

- "Which departments are under the most pressure to do more with less?"
- "Where do you see competitors gaining advantages?"
- "What would happen if [specific department] was 30% more efficient?"

AI Readiness Assessment Pro Tips:

- Focus on time-consuming, repetitive tasks
- Identify tasks requiring writing, research, or analysis
- Look for processes with clear inputs and outputs
- Prioritize departments with measurable outcomes

Red flags to avoid:

- Departments with high regulatory constraints (start elsewhere)
- Teams with resistant leadership
- Areas with complex, custom workflows
- Groups that have recently had major changes

Step 2: Use Case Design and Tool Selection (Week 3-4)

Don't just pick use cases. Design competitive advantages.

Department	High-Impact Use Cases	Business Outcome
Sales	Prospect research, follow-up emails, call summaries	Faster deal cycles, higher conversion
Marketing	Content creation, social posts, campaign analysis, marketing videos	More content, better engagement

Department	High-Impact Use Cases	Business Outcome
HR	Job descriptions, onboarding docs and videos, policy updates	Faster hiring, better retention
Support	Ticket summaries, response drafts, documentation	Faster resolution, higher satisfaction
Finance	Report narratives, budget analysis, data insights	Better decision support, faster reporting

Tool Selection Strategy:

Start with one or two tools maximum per department—any more creates confusion and reduces adoption. Prioritize tools that integrate with existing systems rather than forcing employees to learn entirely new workflows. Choose based on the department's primary output type—writing tools for marketing, research tools for sales, analysis tools for finance. Always consider licensing costs and management complexity because you'll be the one supporting and billing for these tools long-term.

Step 3: Targeted Training and Implementation (Week 5-8)

Department-specific training that drives adoption:

Sales Team Training Framework:

Session 1: Prospect Research Mastery (45 minutes)

- Using Perplexity Pro for competitive intelligence (See Chapter 11 on BSN's deep research prospect prompt)
- Building prospect profiles in 5 minutes vs. 30 minutes
- Identifying conversation starters and pain points

Session 2: Communication Acceleration (45 minutes)

- Follow-up email templates and customization
- Proposal drafting and refinement

- Meeting summary automation

Session 3: Advanced Techniques (30 minutes)

- Objection handling research
- Territory analysis and planning
- CRM integration workflows

HR Team Training Framework:

Session 1: Content Creation Foundations (45 minutes)

- Job description optimization
- Interview question development
- Policy documentation

Session 2: Employee Communication (45 minutes)

- Onboarding material creation
- Performance review assistance
- Internal communication drafting

Session 3: Strategic HR Support (30 minutes)

- Employee survey analysis
- Training material development
- Compliance documentation

Training Success Metrics:

- 90%+ attendance at all sessions
- 80%+ of participants using tools within one week
- 5+ success stories documented within first month

Step 4: Success Measurement and Story Creation (Week 9-12)

Track metrics that matter to leadership. The key is measuring both quantitative results and qualitative wins that you can share with other departments and leadership.

Focus on:

- **Time savings**: How much faster are key tasks?

- **Quality improvement**: Better outcomes, fewer errors

- **Employee satisfaction**: Are people actually using and enjoying the tools?

- **Business impact**: Revenue, efficiency, competitive advantage

For detailed frameworks on measuring AI ROI and creating compelling success metrics, see Chapter 12.

Story Creation Framework

"Before AI: [Specific time/pain point]"

"After AI: [Specific improvement/result]"

"Business Impact: [Revenue/efficiency gain]"

"Employee Reaction: [Quote from user]"

These stories become your most powerful sales tool for expanding to other departments.

Lighthouse Strategy: Turning Wins Into Expansion

Each successful department becomes a lighthouse—a bright example others want to follow.

How to Amplify Lighthouse Success:

Internal Case Study Creation

Document specific time savings and business impact.

Create before/after workflow comparisons.

Gather employee testimonials and quotes.

Quantify ROI and productivity gains.

Leadership Presentation

> Present results to executive team.

> Show departmental success metrics.

> Demonstrate competitive advantages gained.

> Propose expansion to additional departments.

Peer Department Engagement

> Facilitate "lunch and learn" sessions with other departments.

> Have lighthouse team members share their experience.

> Identify next logical department for expansion.

> Begin discovery process for Department #2.

Expansion Sequence Strategy

Each phase builds credibility for the next.

Phase 1

Sales or Marketing (high visibility, quick wins)

Phase 2

HR or Support (operational efficiency)

Phase 3

Finance or Operations (strategic analysis)

Phase 4

Executive/Leadership (strategic planning)

Your Competitive Moat

By the time you've successfully implemented AI in 2-3 departments, you will have proven results (while those consultants only have proposals). You will have fostered internal champions (while your competition only has presentations to offer). And you will have built strategic relationships (while the consultants can only suggest "let's meet").

You will have proven that AI transformation happens through implementation, not consultation.

Best of all? Your MSP will have significant expansion opportunities.

Success Pattern Recognition

Watch for these indicators that you're winning:

Month 1: Department employees actively use tools daily

Month 2: Other departments ask, "How can we get this?"

Month 3: Leadership requests expansion planning

Month 4: Client refers you to other businesses

Month 5: Client sees you as their AI strategic partner

When you see this pattern, you've created a competitive moat that consultants can't easily breach.

Your Role as the Journey Owner

Here's where you add irreplaceable value for your client.

You're facilitating discovery that uncovers real business needs, what's slowing teams down, costing deals, or wasting time, not just selling whatever AI tool is trending.

You're conducting readiness assessments that pinpoint where AI can actually solve problems, not just opportunities to upsell services. This fosters trust and strengthens your credibility as a strategic partner.

You're recommending and implementing tools that fit how the client actually works, not forcing them to change everything for the sake of using AI.

You're delivering practical training that gets employees using these tools effectively, not just checking the box on "AI awareness" with another generic training.

You're measuring and reporting success that proves ROI with real numbers and stories, not vague promises about productivity gains.

And you're planning strategic expansion that grows your relationship while genuinely helping the client improve how they work.

You don't need to be in every meeting, but you should be owning every outcome.

The Bottom Line

Company-wide AI adoption doesn't happen all at once—it happens one department at a time.

Start where the wins are fast and visible. Deliver tools that solve real problems. Train teams in ways that match how they already work. Then track the results, share the stories, and use that momentum to unlock the next department.

This is how AI becomes embedded in the business—not through big launches, but through repeatable impact.

One team. Then two. Then five.

That's the strategy.

And it's how real adoption takes hold.

10

INTERNAL FIRST:

WHY YOUR MSP SHOULD BE USING AI TODAY

Before you help clients adopt AI...

Before you build an AI services stack...

Before you package training or position yourself as a vAIO...

You need to start at home.

Your MSP should be using AI—right now.

This isn't just about "walking the talk." It's about unlocking real productivity inside your business, and creating the experience, stories, and credibility you need to lead clients through the same transformation.

Let's break down how and why to do it.

Why Internal AI Use Is Non-Negotiable

1. You Can't Sell What You Don't Use

Clients will ask how you use AI internally, what's working for your team, and what tools you picked. These aren't casual questions, they're credibility tests. If you don't have real answers, you're just another vendor selling something you've never tried.

However, if you can share specific examples of how AI helps your techs write better documentation, how your sales team researches prospects faster, or how your support team drafts clearer responses, you instantly become trusted.

You're not selling theory. You're sharing experience.

If you don't have answers, you're not credible.

If you do, you're immediately trusted.

2. Your Team Will Become Experts (The Right Way)

The best AI training isn't in a classroom, it's hands-on, daily use. When your staff uses AI every day, they build better prompts through trial and error. They avoid rookie mistakes because they've made them already.

They understand limitations because they've hit them. They get curious about new tools because they see possibilities.

They share wins and teach others because they're excited about what works.

That practical expertise is exactly what clients want in a partner—someone who's walked the path, not just read the map.

3. It Makes Your Business More Efficient

This isn't just about optics. AI will save your team real hours every week.

Your support team can summarize tickets, suggest responses, and route issues based on priority and category instead of reading through every detail manually.

Your techs can convert their technical notes into clear SOPs or client-facing documentation instantly instead of spending hours rewriting everything.

Your account managers can draft emails, security alerts, onboarding guides, and executive summaries faster than ever before.

Your training team can create content or answer staff questions on tools, policies, or platforms without starting from scratch every time.

Marketing can write newsletters three times faster.

Sales will have better insights on prospects through deep research that used to take hours.

Leadership can use AI to draft board updates, analyze contracts, and brainstorm new services without drowning in administrative work.

This is operational excellence that will show up in your margins and your client delivery. When you're more efficient internally, you can invest more time externally... in client success.

How to Roll Out AI Internally (The Strategic Way)

Here's a comprehensive internal adoption plan that addresses real implementation challenges:

Step 1: Executive Mandate + Foundation Setting

Make it clear from the top:

"AI is important. I expect everyone to start experimenting."

Send a company-wide email or announce it at company and/or staff meetings. Get the word out.

But also establish the framework:

- Create an AI Acceptable Use Policy for internal operations
- Set data security boundaries (what never goes into AI)
- Establish quality control standards for AI-assisted work
- Define success metrics and measurement methods

Normalize AI use. Remove fear. But provide structure.

Step 2: Licenses + Policies + Comprehensive Training

- Buy licenses (ChatGPT Teams, Copilot, etc.)
- Distribute an AI Acceptable Use Policy
- Train on what's okay to input, what tools are approved, and how to verify outputs
- **Create role-specific training tracks** based on job functions
- **Establish mentorship pairs** between early adopters and skeptics

Step 3: Role-Based Prompt Guides + Quality Controls

Create a shared document with role-specific examples:

- Sales: "Write a follow-up email to a lead who didn't reply..."
- Marketing: "Draft a blog post about our AI services..."
- Tech: "Summarize this ticket for the client..."
- Ops: "Create a checklist for onboarding a new partner..."

Add quality control checkpoints:

- All client-facing AI content requires human review
- Fact-checking protocols for technical claims
- Peer review for important internal documents

Let people copy and adapt.

Step 4: Weekly Share-Outs + Resistance Management

Hold a short weekly session:

- "Show & Tell: How I Used AI This Week"
- Encourage wins, even small ones
- Highlight creativity, not perfection

These share-outs will help build excitement and momentum.

Address resistance proactively.

The Skeptic: "This is just hype"

- Start with one concrete use case in their daily work
- Pair them with an early adopter for mentoring
- Share specific time-saving examples from their role

The Overwhelmed: "I don't have time to learn this"

- Begin with 5-minute daily experiments
- Provide pre-written prompts for their most common tasks
- Track and celebrate small wins

The Quality Concerned: "AI isn't good enough for our standards"

- Position AI as first draft tool, not final output
- Show side-by-side quality improvements with AI assistance
- Create quality control checklists for AI-assisted work

Step 5: Measurement + Reward Usage

Track meaningful metrics:

Metric	Target	Measurement Method
Tool Adoption Rate	80% weekly usage	License analytics + self-reporting
Time Savings	2-3 hours/week per employee	Before/after task timing
Quality Maintenance	No decrease in client satisfaction	Client feedback scores
Employee Engagement	Increased job satisfaction	Monthly pulse surveys
Innovation Culture	3+ new use cases per month	Share-out session tracking

Then reward the wins! For example, you can:

- Call out great examples in Microsoft Teams or Slack.
- Consider a small prize for "AI Use Case of the Month."

Positive feedback drives adoption.

Client-Facing Integration Strategy

Because you will have direct experience integrating AI in your own business, you can easily position that internal use to drive trust with clients.

During sales conversations, this will enable you to lead the conversation from experience.

> "We use AI daily in our own operations—from research to documentation to client communication drafts. This gives us hands-on experience with both the capabilities and limitations, so we can guide you with real expertise, not just theory."

This will also enable you to preemptively address client concerns. When clients ask: "Are you experimenting on us?" you can confidently respond that you perfect processes internally first, then apply proven methods to client work.

If they worry that quality will suffer, explain that you use AI to enhance human expertise, not replace it. Every output gets human review and verification.

And when they ask about confidentiality, reassure them that you never input client data into AI tools. Your internal use focuses on general processes and research that doesn't involve sensitive information.

What Happens When You Use AI Internally

You get smarter about what works, not from reading articles or watching demos, but from daily experience with tools that solve real problems.

You discover new services to offer clients because you're constantly finding ways AI helps your own operations.

You build a culture of innovation where employees feel empowered to experiment and share discoveries instead of just following the same old processes.

You differentiate your MSP in a crowded market because you can speak from experience, not theory.

You attract talent who want to work with modern tools and cutting-edge technology instead of just managing legacy systems.

Most importantly, when you use AI internally, you become a better advisor because you've lived the journey—you know which tools are overhyped, which prompts actually work, and where clients will inevitably struggle.

This transformation from AI user to AI guide is what separates successful MSPs from those still trying to figure it out.

Internal Use is Your Marketing Engine

Every success story becomes:

- A LinkedIn post
- A client email
- A webinar topic
- A QBR slide
- A case study
- A sales objection crusher

"We use this tool ourselves—here's what we've learned."

That lands. Every time.

Make It Mandatory (Eventually)

You don't need to force adoption on Day 1, but within 60-90 days, AI should be a standard tool in everyone's workflow, not an optional experiment.

Make it part of your employee onboarding so new hires learn AI skills from day one. Discuss AI wins and challenges in weekly team meetings to keep momentum going. Embed AI use into your SOPs so it becomes part of how work gets done, not an add-on task. Measure AI adoption and effectiveness in performance reviews to show it matters. And make basic AI competency a required skill for new hires, just like proficiency in email or Microsoft Office.

You wouldn't let employees skip using email.

AI is next.

Scaling Your AI Culture

New Employee Onboarding

- AI competency assessment during hiring
- Mandatory AI training in first week
- AI usage expectations in job descriptions
- Mentorship program with AI-proficient employees

Growth Management

- Document AI use cases for standardization
- Create role-specific AI competency requirements
- Build AI adoption into performance reviews
- Establish AI innovation time (dedicated experimentation)

Monthly Health Check Framework

Use this simple checklist to track your internal AI adoption progress

---

AI Adoption Health Check

Month: _____

Usage & Adoption:

- Active users: _____% (target: 80%+)

- New use cases this month: _____

- Employee satisfaction trend: ↑   ↓   →

Impact & Quality:

- Client impact (positive/negative): _____

- Quality control incidents:_____

- Success stories documented: _____

Progress & Issues:

- Resistance issues identified: _____

- ROI tracking: On target / Behind / Ahead

- Next month's focus: _____

Complete this monthly to track progress and identify areas needing attention.

Use This for a Client Adoption Playbook

This framework for adoption isn't just for your MSP. It is the exact playbook your clients should use to drive adoption.

Show them your playbook... how it worked, what the results were. Encourage them to use the same for their business and employees.

Your internal adoption journey becomes their implementation roadmap.

The Bottom Line

Internal AI adoption isn't just about using cool tools.

It's about building authentic expertise that clients can trust because you've walked the path yourself. It's about creating competitive differentiation in a crowded market where most MSPs are still figuring out the basics. You'll generate measurable productivity gains for your business that show up in your margins and client delivery. You'll develop success stories that sell themselves because they're real, specific, and relatable. And you'll establish cultural foundations for long-term AI leadership that will serve you as the technology continues to evolve.

Remember: Internal adoption done right becomes your most powerful client acquisition and retention tool.

When you can say...

> **"Here's exactly how we use AI,
> and here's what works, what doesn't,
> and how we've achieved 300% ROI."**

...this won't be a sales pitch. You'll simply be sharing proven results.

Your MSP becomes the case study for successful adoption.

11

Our AI Journey:

How BSN Adopted AI From the Inside Out

We just discussed how you can adopt AI in your MSP. Let's look at how my company, Breach Secure Now (BSN), adopted AI and provide some more clarity.

We didn't just talk about AI. We used it. Every team. Every department. Every week.

This is the real story of how we built an AI-first culture—without an internal IT team, without consultants and without a roadmap.

If we can do it, so can your clients. And so can you.

It Started With Curiosity

Three years ago, I tried ChatGPT for the first time. Within ten minutes, I knew: *This is going to change everything.*

As I mentioned, I've been through every wave—the internet, the cloud, HIPAA, cybersecurity—and nothing has hit me with the same velocity and impact as generative AI.

So I did what I've always done as a CEO: I started shouting from the rooftops.

"Start experimenting. Don't wait. Try it now."

On every company call, I evangelized it.

Top-Down Push. Bottom-Up Excitement

We're a 100-person company. We have Sales, Marketing, Finance, Accounting, Support, Product, Development... just like your clients.

We don't have internal IT. Everything is in the cloud. Everyone runs on laptops. We look a lot like a modern SMB.

And once I saw the power of AI, I pushed adoption from the top down:

- We bought ChatGPT Team and Microsoft Copilot licenses.
- We created an Acceptable Use Policy for AI.
- We built AI Awareness Training programs.
- We set clear expectations:
  "Don't hide your AI use—share it."
- We normalized AI conversations across the business.

Every Friday, we have a collaboration meeting. People show off their latest use cases. The energy is electric!

We created a Microsoft Teams chat just for prompts and articles.

We removed the fear.

We made it fun.

And the results? Game-changing.

Productivity Gains Are Just the Beginning

Let's get the obvious stuff out of the way. Yes, AI made us faster.

Writing scripts for weekly micro-trainings used to eat up two full days of our content team's time. Now? Two hours and we're done.

Reviewing contracts used to mean several hours of line-by-line analysis. Now we get through them in under an hour with AI helping us spot key terms and potential issues.

Drafting blog posts, phishing simulations, or support messages that used to take our team half a day? Way faster now.

But that was only the beginning.

The real transformation wasn't about speed. It was about capability.

AI Helped Us Enter New Markets

We'd been hearing it for a while from our partners:

"Can you help us train our clients on Microsoft 365? They're using the tools—but don't know how."

We knew it was a big opportunity, but internally, none of us were deep Microsoft 365 experts. We used the tools, sure—but not enough to teach them at scale.

Enter ChatGPT.

Suddenly, we had access to a subject matter expert with infinite knowledge of M365. It knew every feature. Every update. Every integration.

We leveraged ChatGPT to:

- Source curriculum knowledge
- Structure lesson outlines
- Speed up scriptwriting
- Generate examples and exercises

Then we layered in our expertise: engaging content, great delivery, and a deep understanding of how SMB employees learn.

The result?

A brand-new training product line, built faster and better than ever.

We Did It Again With AI Awareness

When we built our AI Awareness Training product, guess what helped us with the content?

AI itself.

We used ChatGPT to:

- Identify common risks
- Create role-based use case examples
- Draft content quickly
- Refine scripts and scenarios

And with OSHA

We even used AI to break into more healthcare-specific OSHA training. We didn't have the internal expertise—but AI gave us the foundation.

Here's the key: AI was just the starting point. We hired an OSHA expert to review the content... to fact-check... to refine... to ensure accuracy.

This is our standard practice across all BSN content. AI accelerates creation, but humans ensure credibility. Every training module gets validated by professionals.

Again, this wasn't just about doing things *faster*.

It was about doing things we *couldn't do before*.

Sales Transformed with Perplexity

Here's one of my favorite use cases.

Our sales team—SDRs, account execs, partner managers—talk to dozens of MSPs every week.

They used to prep the old-fashioned way:

- Visit the website
- Skim for insights
- Check LinkedIn
- Piece together context

Now?

They use Perplexity Pro to do deep research on every prospect.

In five minutes, they walk into a call with:

- Insights about the MSP
- Background on the decision-makers
- Context from interviews, press, and 20 other sources

It's like giving your sales team their own researcher. And it works.

Even if we gave them a full week to prep, they couldn't pull off this level of insight.

Here's the modified version of our research prompt that any MSP or SMB can use:

** Begin Prompt **

Deep Research Prompt: SMB Prospect Intelligence Report
(Fill in the initial details before starting your analysis)

Prospect Profile

- Company Name:
- Company Website:
- Main Contact Name:
- Contact Title:
- LinkedIn Profile URL:
- Date of Meeting/Call:

∩structions

Using publicly available sources (company website, LinkedIn, business databases, review platforms, local media, etc.), complete this deep-dive to build a full picture of the SMB prospect. The goal is to understand their identity, momentum, challenges, digital maturity, and competitive position—so your team can approach with maximum relevance and credibility.

1. Company Overview

- When was the company founded?
- What is their ownership structure? (Private, family-owned, franchise, recently acquired, etc.)
- What products/services do they offer?
- What are their primary customer segments (B2B, B2C, hybrid)?
- Where do they operate geographically? (Local, regional, national, global)
- Any recent signs of growth or momentum? (e.g., hiring, expansion, new product lines, capital investment)

2. Contact Person Analysis

- What is the background and role of the key contact?
- Are they a founder, executive, department head, or operational lead?
- What types of content do they engage with publicly (LinkedIn posts, articles, podcasts, etc.)?
- Do they show interest in topics like growth, automation, AI, marketing, or team building?
- Do they appear to be a key decision-maker or an internal influencer?

3. Website & Digital Presence

- Is the website modern, fast, and mobile-optimized?
- Is the company's value proposition clear and prominent?
- Do they explain what differentiates them from competitors?
- Are there visible calls-to-action (contact forms, lead magnets, offers)?
- Is there a blog or resource hub? Is it active and up to date?
- Do they highlight digital tools, automation, AI, or customer portals?

4. Services, Offerings, and Positioning

- What specific services or product lines are most prominently featured?

- Do they bundle or cross-sell offerings?
- Do they target a premium, mid-market, or budget-conscious buyer?
- Are there opportunities for value-added services, strategic advice, or partnerships?

5. Competitor Landscape

- Identify 2–3 direct competitors (local or national, depending on their scope).
- Compare competitors' service offerings, branding, and differentiation.
- How does this company stand out—or fall short—compared to competitors?
- Are there indirect competitors disrupting their space (e.g., DIY platforms, online alternatives)?

6. Business Trends & Environmental Factors

- What external trends or market forces likely impact their business (e.g., AI, labor shifts, regulations, digital transformation, supply chain, cybersecurity)?
- How might these trends create opportunities or pressure for this company?
- Are there signs they're adopting (or resisting) these changes?
- What's their potential risk exposure to emerging tech or economic factors?

7. SWOT Analysis — Prospect Company

Strengths:
Weaknesses:
Opportunities:
Threats:

8. SWOT Snapshot — Key Competitor

Strengths:
Weaknesses:
Opportunities:
Threats:

9. Reputation, Reviews & Public Perception

- What are customers saying on Google, Yelp, industry directories, or news articles?

- Are there patterns in praise or complaints (e.g., slow service, great quality, unresponsive support)?
- Any awards, press, or recognition worth noting?
- Are they active in community involvement, associations, or thought leadership?

10. Red Flags or Strategic Triggers

- Have there been leadership changes, restructuring, funding events, or legal issues?
- Are there signs of operational stress (e.g., hiring delays, low Glassdoor scores, vendor churn)?
- Are they entering a phase that might trigger new needs—expansion, rebranding, digital overhaul, or compliance?
- Any early signals that a service like yours would solve an urgent need?

Final Summary & Go-To-Market Angle

Write 2–3 concise sentences explaining:

- Why this SMB is a promising prospect
- What their top 1–2 challenges or opportunities appear to be
- The strategic angle your team should lead with (e.g., growth enablement, operational efficiency, compliance readiness, digital modernization)

** End Prompt **

This is a modified version of the prompt we use internally at BSN for researching MSP prospects. We've adapted it to work for any business type, and you can customize it further for your specific industry or service offerings.

Share this with your clients—it's a game-changer for any sales team doing prospect research.

The Prompt in Use

To show you how powerful this research prompt is, I ran it on my own company, Breach Secure Now. Here's a portion of what it generated in just a few minutes:

Breach Secure Now — SMB Prospect Intelligence (Sample)

1 Company Overview

Founded in 2010 and headquartered in Morristown, New Jersey, Breach Secure Now (BSN) provides cybersecurity-focused training and compliance solutions to small and mid-sized businesses through a channel-only strategy that serves managed service providers (MSPs) nationwide.

2 Products & Services

BSN positions itself as the "channel leader in Cybersecurity Awareness, AI Awareness & HIPAA Compliance training" for MSPs. Core offerings include:

- AI Awareness Training – Comprehensive generative AI fundamentals, cybersecurity training, and BSN's exclusive Generative AI Certification Program designed to help MSPs lead strategic AI conversations with clients
- Continuous cybersecurity-awareness training with simulated phishing
- HIPAA compliance education and documentation tools for healthcare clients
- Dark-web monitoring with automated breach alerts
- Security-risk assessments and policy templates
- Microsoft 365 productivity training modules

The AI Awareness Training component includes several key elements:

- AI Fundamentals – 20-minute course covering generative AI, chatbots like ChatGPT, definitions, applications, and ethical considerations
- AI Cybersecurity Training – 15-minute overview of AI's role in cybersecurity, highlighting threats and best practices for identifying AI-generated scams

- AI Nanos© – Ultra-compact, sub-60-second videos providing quick tips and tricks for mastering AI

- AI Fundamentals Guidebook – Downloadable resource with detailed insights into AI concepts and the CHAT method for prompt creation

- AI Acceptable Use Policy Template – Guidelines for ethical AI use, ensuring compliance with legal standards

- Generative AI Certification Program – Industry-first certification exclusively for MSPs, helping them lead strategic AI conversations and position themselves as trusted AI advisors

This AI training suite is integrated into BSN's Breach Prevention & Productivity (BPP) platform and represents their expansion beyond traditional cybersecurity into the rapidly growing AI awareness market.

3 Growth & Momentum Indicators

- Rapid adoption of the new *Generative AI Awareness* course has expanded BSN's training suite beyond traditional security topics.

- Platform integration with Microsoft Teams shows measurable improvements in user "Employee Secure Scores (ESS)," highlighting product impact.

- Consistent publication of webinars, white-label content, and partner marketing kits signals ongoing investment in channel enablement.

4 Contact Person Analysis – Art Gross (CEO)

Art Gross is the founder-CEO of BSN and of sister IT services firm Entegration, Inc. With more than three decades in enterprise and healthcare IT, he regularly shares thought leadership on LinkedIn about MSP business evolution, cybersecurity best practices, and—most recently—the commercial potential of generative AI. Gross is therefore both strategic decision-maker and public face of the company, actively shaping BSN's product roadmap and market positioning.

5 Website & Digital Presence

The BSN website is fast, mobile-responsive, and branded around the tagline *"Making Humans Super."* Key observations:

- Clear MSP-focused value proposition above the fold

- Prominent calls-to-action for partnership demos and resource downloads

- Active blog and on-demand webinar library, updated monthly
- Emphasis on automation features (e.g., phishing campaigns, reporting dashboards) and emerging tech topics like AI safety

6 Services, Offerings & Positioning

BSN sells an integrated platform that bundles security, AI awareness, productivity, and compliance content for MSP resale. Positioning highlights:

- Channel exclusivity—no direct-to-end-customer sales
- Add-on modules (AI, M365, HIPAA) that enable MSPs to upsell broader "human layer" training
- Competitive pricing designed for margin-positive resale while undercutting enterprise-oriented vendors

7 Reputation, Reviews & Public Perception

Discussion threads in MSP-focused Reddit forums and peer groups describe BSN as a *cost-effective* and *MSP-friendly* alternative to larger security-awareness vendors, frequently citing:

- Responsive support and onboarding
- Comprehensive policy-template library
- Easy-to-read phishing and dark-web reports for end clients
- Overall sentiment skews positive, with partners emphasizing BSN's channel commitment and steady feature rollouts.

8 Final Summary

Breach Secure Now is a proven, channel-exclusive training provider that has differentiated itself by expanding quickly into AI and productivity enablement while maintaining strong MSP support infrastructure. Its focus on the "human element" of security, AI, M365 and compliance, combined with a founder-led culture of continuous innovation, makes BSN a relevant prospect for solutions or partnerships aligned with MSP growth and end-user education.

The Culture Shift Is the Real Win

Yes, we saw productivity gains. Yes, we launched new products. Yes, we improved sales research and support efficiency.

But the biggest win?

Culture.

AI became part of how we work. Every employee feels empowered to explore. No one hides their AI use.

People share wins. They share prompts.

They ask questions. They cheer each other on.

That's what adoption looks like.

And it didn't take an enterprise platform, consultants, or full-time AI staff. It took *executive support, structured encouragement,* and a *willingness to learn.*

Why This Matters for MSPs

I'm telling you this because I want you to see what's possible.

BSN is a modern SMB. We weren't experts in AI. We just leaned in. And the payoff was huge!

You can do the same for your business.

More importantly? You can help your clients do it too.

The Bottom Line

AI didn't just save us time.

It helped us:

- Build things we never could before
- Launch new offerings
- Transform our sales process
- Empower every employee
- Create a culture of innovation

If you're waiting for perfection before adopting AI?

Don't.

Progress beats perfection.

Your clients don't need you to be an expert. They need a guide.

And the best way to guide them? Start walking the path yourself.

We did. And it's been the most exciting—and valuable—transformation we've ever made.

Now it's your turn.

12

MEASURING THE ROI OF GENERATIVE AI

Let's get to the question every SMB client eventually asks:

"If I'm paying $30/month per employee for AI tools, and more for your MSP to help, how much is this actually saving me? Is it worth it?"

Fair question.

And here's the uncomfortable truth: Measuring ROI from generative AI isn't as cut and dry as we'd like it to be. But that doesn't mean it can't be done.

Let's break it down simply.

The Illusion of Easy ROI

On paper, it sounds simple:

- Before AI: A task takes 4 hours.
- After AI: It takes 2 hours.
- ROI: 2 hours saved × hourly wage = Value.

But there's a catch.

Most businesses don't track how long tasks take in the first place. And employees aren't clocking in and out of every proposal, blog post, or sales follow-up they create.

So when AI shortens a task, we're often guessing at how much time it actually saved.

That's not unique to AI. It's been the same with every productivity tool we've introduced—from Excel to Salesforce to Teams.

Which means we need a smarter, simpler way to demonstrate value.

Let's Talk About Microsoft 365

Everyone wants to measure the ROI of AI. I get it. It's new, hyped, and promising massive productivity gains. Business owners want to see the dollars saved.

But here's a question:

When was the last time you calculated the ROI of Microsoft 365?

How much time or money does a spreadsheet in Excel save you? How much faster is a deal closed because of Outlook or Teams? How much value does a Word doc or PowerPoint really add?

We don't know. And we don't try. Because M365 is just part of how business gets done. It's embedded infrastructure. We assume it makes work better—because it does.

AI is following that same path.

Right now, it's still novel. People want proof. But soon, tools like ChatGPT and Copilot will be as expected as Excel. You won't ask, "What's the ROI of AI?" any more than you ask, "What's the ROI of spell check?"

That doesn't mean the question isn't valid. I'd love a clean ROI report for every M365 license I pay for. But I don't need one to know that without it, our productivity would crash.

Same with AI.

So, yes—ask the question. Track usage. Gather stories. Measure what you can.

Just don't forget: Real ROI shows up when people have the right tools in their hands. And that's always worth it.

So if we know AI delivers value—but it's tough to quantify like M365—how do we measure just enough to keep clients confident? Start simple.

Start Simple: Just Ask Employees

The most direct method?

Just ask.

- "Has AI helped you save time?"

- "Roughly how many hours per week?"

- "Which tasks are faster now?"

- "What can you do now that you couldn't before?"

This might sound subjective, and it is. But it's also one of the most revealing data points you'll get.

It's the same reason companies use Net Promoter Score (NPS)[2] to measure customer satisfaction. It's not perfect, but it's simple, scalable, and provides directional insight.

We can do the same for AI.

The AI ROI Score (AIRS): Keep It Simple

Imagine a quick, 3-question survey employees complete monthly:

1. "Do AI tools help you save time at work?" (Yes/No)

---

[2] Net Promoter Score (NPS) is a metric used to measure customer loyalty and is a gauge of how likely customers are to recommend a company's products or services to others. It's calculated by asking customers a single question: "How likely are you to recommend [company] to a friend or colleague?" on a scale of 0 to 10. The score is then calculated by subtracting the percentage of "detractors" (those who rate 0-6) from the percentage of "promoters" (those who rate 9 or 10).

2. "How much time are you saving per week on average?" (Multiple choice: 0–1 hr, 1–3 hrs, 3–5 hrs, 5+ hrs)

3. "Which task types are you using AI for most?" (Writing, research, summarization, brainstorming, etc.)

Roll those responses up across a company and you get a clear, repeatable signal:

- Who's seeing value
- Where they're seeing it
- How widespread AI adoption is becoming

And most importantly, you get a number your clients can track over time.

That's it. Nothing fancy. Nothing complex.

Usage = Value

Here's another data point that matters:

Tool usage.

If someone isn't opening ChatGPT, Copilot, or Perplexity, they're not getting value. But if someone is in those tools daily—creating, asking, exploring—that's a strong proxy for ROI.

Start tracking:

- Logins per week
- Time spent in tool
- Number of prompts submitted

These are objective signals of engagement. And engagement precedes ROI.

No usage? No savings.

As mentioned in Chapter 2, many AI tools don't provide detailed information on usage. Let's hope this changes in the future.

The tools that do (Copilot, which is limited, and ChatGPT enterprise) can help with this metric. Without this data, adding another question to the 3-question survey can help:

- How much do you use AI in a week?
  (Multiple choice: 0–1 hr, 1–5 hrs, 5–7 hrs, 10+ hrs)

Actual data is better. But without it, this question helps.

Training = More Value

The more employees train, the more they get out of the tools.

Think of Excel. Giving someone Excel without teaching them formulas, pivot tables, or data tools is like giving them a racecar with no instruction manual.

That car is not moving.

Same goes for AI.

Track:

- Number of training sessions attended
- AI certifications completed
- Engagement with prompt libraries or workshops

More training → better prompting → more efficiency → higher ROI.

Simple.

Collect Real Stories (The Most Powerful ROI)

Numbers are good. Stories are better.

Start collecting specific examples:

- "Our HR manager used to spend 3 hours writing job descriptions. Now it takes 30 minutes."

- "Sales team research that took half a day now takes 10 minutes."

- "We can create a month's worth of social media content in 2 hours instead of 2 days."

These stories do three things:

1. **They're relatable**: Other employees see how peers are winning

2. **They're memorable**: Leadership remembers stories better than statistics

3. **They're shareable**: You can use them with other clients

Collect 2-3 new stories every month. That's your most powerful ROI data.

Simple Monthly Dashboard

Put it all together in a simple dashboard:

```
AI Adoption Health Check
Month: _____
Usage:
    • % of employees using AI weekly:    ___
    • Average usage hours per week:      ___
Satisfaction:
    • % reporting time savings:          ___
    • Average hours saved per week:      ___
Training:
    • Employees trained this month:      ___
    • Training sessions completed:       ___
Success Stories:
    • Story 1: _____
    • Story 2: _____
    • Story 3: _____
Next Month's Focus:
    • _____
```

That's it. One page. Five minutes to complete. Powerful insight.

The "Good Enough" ROI Calculation

If clients push for numbers, here's the simplest calculation that works:

Step 1: Survey says employees save an average of 3 hours/week

Step 2: 10 employees × 3 hours = 30 hours/week saved

Step 3: 30 hours × $25/hour = $750/week value

Step 4: $750/week × 50 weeks = $37,500/year value

Step 5: AI costs = $3,600/year ($30/month × 10 employees) + MSP AI management and training costs: $2,400/year ($20/month × 10 employees)

Step 6: ROI = $37,500 / $6,000 = 525%

Is this perfect? No. Is this directionally accurate? Yes. Is this good enough to justify AI investment? Absolutely.

Why This Matters for MSPs

Clients don't just want to "try" AI. They want results.

If you can be the partner who not only introduces AI safely, but also tracks and reports on ROI, you instantly differentiate yourself.

You're not just selling tools.

You're delivering outcomes.

And you're doing it with simple, believable methods that don't require a data science degree.

Better ROI Tools Are Coming—But Don't Wait

AI analytics are catching up fast. Copilot is adding better reporting. ChatGPT Enterprise already gives you usage stats the free and Team versions don't

Soon, you'll start seeing deeper insights—how long users spend in tools, which prompts drive the most value, even quality scores on AI-generated content.

As AI becomes embedded in workflows, more vendors will roll out real ROI dashboards with things like cross-platform usage data, automation impact, productivity trends, and industry benchmarks.

Think of it like what happened with cybersecurity reporting—basic at first, then mature and MSP-friendly.

But here's the key: Don't wait for perfect tools. Start measuring what you can today. Build trust with simple reporting.

When the advanced platforms show up, you'll already have the habit, and the credibility, to make the most of them.

"Good enough" beats "nothing at all." Every time.

The Quality Factor (Hard to Measure, Easy to See)

Here's what most ROI calculations miss: Quality.

AI doesn't just make things faster. It makes things better.

Think about it:

- Clearer writing: AI helps employees communicate more professionally
- Better research: Perplexity finds sources your team would never discover
- Deeper analysis: AI helps spot patterns in data humans miss

But how do you measure "better"?

You don't. You notice it.

...When a sales rep walks into a call with insights they couldn't have found manually.

...When marketing creates content that actually engages customers.

...When support tickets get resolved with solutions that actually work.

That's quality improvement. And it's real value.

Even if you can't put a dollar sign on it.

So when you're talking ROI with clients, don't forget: "AI isn't just saving time. It's improving outcomes."

Some wins you measure. Some wins you just celebrate.

The Bottom Line

Perfect AI ROI measurement doesn't exist. But meaningful insight does.

You don't need complex ROI calculations to prove AI value today.

You need:

- Employee feedback that shows satisfaction
- Usage data that shows adoption
- Stories that show real impact
- Simple numbers that show directional value

When you provide this consistently, monthly reports, quarterly summaries, real examples, you move from "AI vendor" to "AI enabler." You're helping clients see that AI isn't an expense, it's an investment that pays for itself in the first month.

And as the measurement tools evolve, you'll be positioned to provide even more sophisticated ROI analysis while your competitors are still figuring out the basics.

Start simple today. Scale with better tools tomorrow. Lead the entire journey.

That's how you win the ROI conversation without becoming a data scientist, and maintain your competitive advantage as the measurement landscape matures.

13

SELLING AI SERVICES:

PRICING, PACKAGING, AND POSITIONING

So you believe in AI.

You've tested tools. You've trained employees. You're ready to bring AI to your clients.

Now comes the big question:

"How do I actually sell this?"

This chapter gives you the practical frameworks to price, package, and position AI services—so you can turn insight into income.

Step 1: Understand What SMBs Will Actually Pay For

Think about how you sell Microsoft 365.

When you sell Microsoft 365, SMBs aren't looking for:

- Advanced Excel training or macro development
- Custom SharePoint site designs
- Complex Power Platform automations
- Deep OneDrive architecture consulting

What they *do* pay you for with M365:

- The right licensing for their needs
- Secure setup and configuration
- Employee training so they can actually use the tools
- Ongoing support when things don't work
- Guidance on which features matter for their business

AI works exactly the same way.

SMBs are not looking for:

- Technical AI audits
- Custom GPT builds
- Long AI strategy documents

What they *will* pay for:

- Training that protects them from risk
- Tools that help employees get more done
- Support that makes AI adoption feel safe and easy
- Simple ways to measure ROI
- Guidance they can trust

So your job is to take the services you can deliver, and wrap them in outcomes.

Just like you position M365 as "productivity and collaboration tools that work securely"... position AI as "the AI intern that makes every employee more effective."

Step 2: Create Tiered Offerings

Anchor your pricing to what they already know.

Your clients already pay for:

- Microsoft 365 licenses ($6-55/user/month)
- Cybersecurity training ($3-8/user/month)
- Cloud backup services ($5-15/user/month)
- vCIO hours ($150-300/hour)

So anchor your AI services to what they know:

"This is like M365 support,
but for your digital workforce."

"Think of it like Security Awareness Training
but focused on safe AI use."

"We're your Virtual AI Officer,
just like we're your Virtual CIO."

Here's a simple 3-tier structure:

Note: The pricing below covers MSP services only and does not include AI tool licensing costs (ChatGPT Team, Copilot, etc.), which are billed separately.

Tier 1: Foundational – "AI Starter Pack"

Like M365 Business Basic—gets you started safely

Best for: SMBs just starting their journey

What's included:

- Guided internal AI adoption support
- Ongoing AI awareness training (live or on-demand)
- Prompt library by role
- Acceptable Use Policy template
- AI readiness assessment
- Basic provisioning support for ChatGPT, Copilot, etc.
- Monthly "What's New in AI" update email

Price: $500–$1,500 flat or $5-$10/employee per month

Position it like: "Basic M365 licensing—we get you set up safely, trained, and help you adopt AI successfully."

Guided Internal AI Adoption Support

The AI Starter Pack isn't just about tools and training—it's about helping your client roll out AI internally using the same proven framework you used for your own MSP (detailed in Chapter 10). This strategic rollout ensures effective adoption rather than chaotic experimentation.

Here's how you guide their internal adoption:

Step 1: Executive Foundation. You'll help leadership craft the "AI is important" message for their team and assist with company-wide communication about AI expectations. Working closely with management, you'll establish their AI Acceptable Use Policy and set clear data security boundaries.

Step 2: Structured Rollout. You'll guide tool selection, license procurement, and provisioning, then deliver comprehensive ongoing training that covers approved tools, safe usage practices, and role-specific applications. This includes help establishing mentorship pairs between early adopters and hesitant employees while creating human review requirements for AI-assisted work.

Step 3: Role-Based Implementation. You'll develop customized prompt guides for their specific departments (sales, marketing, support, etc.) and establish review processes for client-facing AI content. The focus is on creating job-relevant examples employees can immediately use in their daily work.

Step 4: Culture Building. You'll facilitate "AI wins" sharing sessions and help address resistance from skeptical, overwhelmed, or quality-concerned employees. The goal is to encourage experimentation while maintaining professional standards and building enthusiasm across the organization.

Step 5: Measurement & Momentum. You'll track adoption rates, time savings, and employee satisfaction while celebrating and incentivizing early wins to build momentum. Monthly progress reports to leadership ensure visibility into the AI adoption journey and demonstrate ongoing value.

This isn't just "here are some tools"—it's a complete adoption strategy that ensures your client's AI investment actually gets used effectively and safely. The same framework that worked for your MSP becomes their roadmap to success.

Why clients pay for this assistance: Most businesses struggle with AI adoption because they lack a structured approach. Without guidance, employees either avoid the tools entirely, use them unsafely, or get frustrated and give up. Your proven framework eliminates these problems, ensuring their AI investment delivers real ROI instead of sitting unused. This strategic support—turning AI licensing costs into actual productivity gains—is exactly why clients value your expertise and are willing to pay for your guidance.

For complete implementation details, see Chapter 10: Internal First.

Tier 2: Enablement – "AI Rollout Kit"

Like M365 Business Standard—full productivity features

Best for: Clients ready to empower teams

What's included:

- Everything in Starter Pack
- Department-specific training sessions (Sales, HR, Marketing)
- Quarterly AI Coaching Call
- AI Prompt Playbook customization
- AI Usage Dashboard (report on adoption, wins and basic ROI)

Price: $1,500–$3,500 setup + $10-$20/employee per month

Position it like: "Full M365 with training and support—we help you get the most from your investment."

Tier 3: Strategic – "Virtual AI Officer (vAIO)"

Like M365 E5 + vCIO services—enterprise-level guidance

Best for: Clients who want ongoing transformation

What's included:

- Monthly AI review and roadmap
- Hands-on use case development
- Workflow automation pilots
- Team training refreshers
- Tool evaluations and recommendations

- Detailed ROI reporting

Price: Custom; $1,000–$5,000/month based on scope

Position it like: "Premium M365 with dedicated strategic consulting—we become your AI strategy partner."

Step 3: Use Familiar Language

Don't say: *"We'll implement AI governance frameworks with comprehensive prompt engineering."*

Say: "We'll set up AI tools just like we set up your Microsoft 365—securely, with the right permissions, and with training so your team can actually use them."

Don't say: *"We offer AI transformation consulting."*

Say: "We help you adopt AI the same way we helped you move to the cloud—safely, step by step, with ongoing support."

The Comparison That Seals the Deal

"You probably remember when you first got Microsoft 365. Maybe some people used it, others didn't. Some departments flew ahead, others lagged behind. Sound familiar?

That's exactly what's happening with AI right now in your business.

Just like we helped you get the most from your M365 investment—training your team, setting up security, making sure everyone was productive—we can do the same thing with AI.

Same approach. Same partnership. Next level of capability."

Pricing Psychology That Works

Bundle with existing services:

- "Add AI enablement to your current vCIO package for $X/month"

- "Include AI training with your Security Awareness Training for just $X more per user"

- "AI support is included in your comprehensive managed services agreement"

Use per-user pricing they understand:

- "AI enablement: $10/user/month—about the same as your M365 Business Standard licenses"

- "Less than what you spend on coffee per employee, but with much bigger impact"

Reference familiar ROI:

- "Remember how M365 paid for itself in productivity gains? AI does the same thing, just faster."

- "If your team saves 2 hours per week with AI tools, that's already a 300% ROI on the licensing costs."

This approach makes AI feel like the natural next step in their technology journey, not a scary leap into the unknown.

Step 4: Sell the Outcome, Not the Tool

Don't say: *"We'll set up ChatGPT Team."*

Say: "We'll help your employees write better, research faster, and reclaim 5+ hours/week—with secure, approved AI tools."

Don't say: *"We're offering AI consulting."*

Say: "We help your business unlock productivity with AI—safely, efficiently, and with full employee buy-in."

Sell the win.

Step 5: Use Your Own MSP as the Case Study

Nothing sells better than proof.

Show your prospects:

- How your team uses AI daily
- Where it saves time
- What tools you chose (and why)
- Your internal Acceptable Use Policy
- Prompt examples your techs, ops, and salespeople use
- How you're staying secure while being innovative

You are your best marketing asset.

You are proof that AI adoption isn't difficult and you can show results.

That's gold!

For detailed guidance on implementing AI internally in your MSP, see Chapter 10: Internal First.

Overcoming Common Objections

When they say:

   "We're not ready for AI."

Answer:

   "That's exactly why we start with training and a risk review—so you can experiment safely and get quick wins."

When they say:

"It feels risky."

Answer:

> "We provide guardrails: approved tools, clear policies, and education for your team. You stay in control."

When they say:

"We don't have budget."

Answer:

> "Many clients use their training or technology enablement budget. Start with a small pilot, ROI shows up fast."

When they say:

"What if we don't see value or use it?"

Answer:

> "That's why our AI services are month-to-month, just like your other managed services. No long-term contracts, no big upfront investments. If it's not working after 90 days, you can pause or adjust. But most clients see results within the first month."

When they say:

"We don't want to get locked into something expensive."

Answer:

> "Unlike AI consultants who want 6-12 month contracts, we structure this like your other IT services—flexible, scalable, and designed to grow with your needs. Start small, see results, then expand when you're ready."

When they say:

"Won't this replace employees?"

Answer:

"No, AI helps your employees become more productive. Those who use it best will become your top performers."

Marketing Tactics That Work

- **AI Readiness Assessment**
  Offer it as a free or paid diagnostic

- **Live Webinars or Lunch-and-Learns**
  "AI for [Industry]" or "The Truth About AI Risk"

- **Client Stories**
  Share before/after productivity wins

- **AI Use Case Library**
  Publish a PDF of how real SMBs are using AI

- **Weekly AI Tip Email**
  Build authority and trust over time

- **Onboarding Bundles**
  Include AI training in new client onboarding

These are the same tactics that we used when we rolled out Security Awareness Training and introduced cybersecurity to clients.

It worked back then, and it will work for AI now.

You Don't Need to Monetize Everything on Day 1

Don't feel pressured to productize every service right away.

Start with:

- Training
- Policies
- Provisioning support
- Strategic advice during QBRs

The Foundation, AI Starter Pack is an excellent way to get clients started with AI experimentation

Then layer on:

- AI-enabled workflows
- Automation pilots
- vAIO subscriptions

AI revenue will follow AI leadership.

Start with value, price for outcomes to build trust, and grow over time.

14

FROM GUIDANCE TO LEADERSHIP: EVOLVING INTO THE vAIO ROLE

Up until now, most of what we've talked about has focused on how to help clients *start* their AI journey: raising awareness about risks and opportunities, training employees about safe and effective use, writing policies that encourage experimentation while managing risk, recommending tools that fit their specific needs, and supporting early use cases that prove value quickly.

These are critical first steps.

But once your clients have taken those steps—once they've rolled out some licenses, delivered training, and seen a few early wins—they'll start asking a new question:

"What comes next?"

That's your moment to evolve.

Just like MSPs evolved from implementing basic cybersecurity services to delivering vCISO services... now's the time to evolve from "AI helper" to "AI leader."

That's where the vAIO comes in.

What Is the vAIO?

You've probably heard the term vCIO—Virtual Chief Information Officer.

Or the vCISO—Virtual Chief Information Security Officer.

MSPs have used these for years to add strategic value beyond break/fix. vCIOs and vCISOs help clients plan tech investments, align IT with business goals, align cybersecurity investment, and guide long-term decisions.

Now, a new role is emerging:

vAIO – Virtual AI Officer

And MSPs are perfectly positioned to fill it.

Just like vCIOs and vCISOs led the cloud and cybersecurity transformations, vAIOs will lead the AI transformation.

The **vAIO**—Virtual AI Officer—is the next evolution.

Basic AI services include managing licenses or conducting training. vAIO services are about guiding long-term AI adoption with structure, strategy, and measurable outcomes.

The vAIO isn't for every client.

It's not for day-one adopters. It's for clients who are *already experimenting, already seeing results,* and ready to go deeper.

It's the natural next step.

This chapter shows you how to build, brand, and deliver vAIO services that generate value—and recurring revenue.

Why the vAIO Is a Next-Step Service
(Not a Starting Point)

You can't sell a vCISO service to a client who doesn't care about cybersecurity.

You can't sell vCIO services to a business that still buys tech at Staples.

And you shouldn't try to sell vAIO services to a client who hasn't trained their team, deployed any AI tools, or experienced success.

vAIO is *step two*.

Initial AI adoption is step one. Once the groundwork is in place—tools, policies, habits—the real transformation begins.

That's when clients need structured support to go further.

What Does a vAIO Actually Do?

A strong vAIO service includes:

1. Strategic Guidance

- Help define AI goals per department
- Prioritize use cases by department
- Align AI with business objectives

2. Tool Curation and Re-Evaluation

- Ongoing evaluation of new tools and models
- Recommend upgrades or alternatives
- Align tools with emerging use cases

Tools evolve daily and weekly.

Being able to recommend the best tools for your client is one of the most valuable services you can offer.

Tool selection is not a one-time process. There are new tools, new functionality, new features that unlock endless productivity gains.

That is why this is so important, and a valuable service of the vAIO.

3. Governance and Compliance

- Review and evolve Acceptable Use Policies

- Create/refine data classification guidelines – what data is allowed or restricted in the AI tools? What data can AI tools access and what is restricted? Think of this the same way you think of M365 data classification.

- Ensure regulatory alignment (HIPAA, GDPR, PCI, FTC AI rule, etc.)

4. Cultural Enablement

- Help build a culture of AI adoption – this is critical. Your MSP already has (will have) a culture of AI adoption, show your clients how you enabled it.
- Expand training to new hires
- Refresh content and prompt libraries
- Run "AI Sprints" and office hours
- Normalize cross-department AI sharing
- Create an internal champion program

5. Process Optimization

- Identify repetitive workflows to automate
- Build prompt playbooks mapped to SOPs
- Create lightweight GPTs for recurring tasks

6. Measurement and Reporting

- Track usage and adoption
- Measure ROI
- Surface wins and success stories
- Provide leadership with quarterly impact reviews

This is the strategic layer on top of the enablement foundation you've already built.

Your deliverables might include:

Deliverable	Frequency
AI Roadmap	Quarterly
AI Usage Report	Monthly
Prompt Library Updates	Monthly
Department Deep Dives	Rotational
Training Sessions	Ongoing
Q&A Office Hours	Monthly

Price based on size and complexity. Most SMBs can start with $1,000–$3,000/month.

Align your pricing with what you charge for vCIO or vCISO services.

How to Introduce the vAIO Service

Don't make it a cold pitch.

Instead, position it like this:

> "You've done the hard part. You've trained your employees, rolled out AI tools, and already seen success. But now the questions are piling up.
>
> How do we get more value? How do we make sure we're not falling behind? How do we scale this safely and strategically?
>
> That's exactly what our vAIO service is designed to help with."

You're not selling a new product. *You're unlocking the next level.*

How to Know a Client Is Ready for vAIO Services

Look for signs like:

- They've bought licenses beyond just one or two power users
- Their department heads are asking for guidance
- They're experimenting in Sales, Marketing, HR, or Support
- They've asked you to help write policies or deliver custom training
- They're trying to measure ROI

In short: they've moved beyond curiosity and want to operationalize AI.

That's when vAIO becomes a no-brainer.

Don't Overcomplicate It

You're not building GPT agents from scratch. You're not coding custom automations (yet). You're guiding, advising, and supporting structured AI adoption.

This is the same motion you've already mastered with vCIO and cybersecurity services:

- You align tools to goals
- You reduce risk
- You enable productivity
- You report outcomes

What's changed? The tools are newer, the potential is greater, and the pace of transformation is accelerating.

The Bottom Line

vAIO services is not where you start. It's where you go once your clients trust you to lead.

You earn that trust by helping them succeed with the basics, like comprehensive training that gets employees using AI effectively, policy development that manages risk while encouraging innovation, tool selection and implementation that fits their workflows, and early use cases that deliver quick wins and build confidence.

Then you build on that foundation with ongoing enablement that keeps teams current as tools evolve, clear reporting that proves ROI and tracks adoption, strategic guidance that aligns AI with business goals, and workflow optimization that turns AI from helpful tool into competitive advantage.

It's a natural evolution of the services you already provide—centered on AI. And it's exactly what your most forward-thinking clients will need next.

A Word of Caution

You don't have to rush into vAIO services.

Getting your clients using AI and seeing benefits is a key first step. It builds trust. And it positions you as their AI advisor.

As your MSP becomes more comfortable with AI—analyzing client workflows and recommending AI enhancements to how your clients work—then vAIO services will be a natural progression.

Think about your cybersecurity journey. You started slow with SAT, Dark Web, EDRs and then you got more comfortable.

Maybe you are selling vCISO services now. You didn't at first but your skill set and services evolved over time.

The same will happen with vAIO services.

15

WHAT COMES AFTER THE vAIO?

EVOLVING YOUR AI SERVICES

Let's be honest. I don't know exactly what comes next. And neither does anyone else.

Because we're in the early innings of AI adoption. The landscape is shifting daily. New tools are launching. New capabilities are emerging. And the road beyond six months feels more like science fiction than roadmap.

What I do know is this: If you're building AI services today, if you're helping clients adopt, train, and operationalize AI, then you are perfectly positioned for wherever this goes.

Because AI *will* change the world. It will reshape how MSPs deliver support. It will redefine the services clients expect.

The Unfolding Future of AI for MSPs

There's a lot of buzz right now... AI agents that can talk to other agents. Autonomous workflows that redesign themselves. Voice interfaces that feel like Jarvis from Iron Man. AI-generated podcasts, video content, and deep research in minutes.

It is almost surreal and hard to wrap your head around the capabilities. But it's already starting to happen.

In the same ways the internet unlocked unimaginable access, and cybersecurity gave rise to an entire industry of tools and frameworks, AI will unlock entirely new productivity layers—and business outcomes we can't even conceive of yet.

The best part? MSPs are already in position to lead.

The Parallel: Cybersecurity's Evolution

Think back to when MSPs first began offering cybersecurity. The stack was small:

- Firewalls
- Antivirus
- Security Awareness Training
- Dark Web Monitoring

That was the beginning. But soon came:

- EDRs and MDRs
- SOCs and SIEMs
- vCISOs and compliance frameworks
- Cyber insurance, frameworks, and layered defenses

The stack exploded.

AI will follow the same path.

Today's services—training, prompting help, usage dashboards, vAIO consulting—are just the beginning.

What's coming next?

- AI security stack integration
- Shadow AI detection and risk management
- Prompt libraries-as-a-service
- AI policy compliance frameworks
- Automation mapping
- Cross-AI agent orchestration
- Channel vendors that merge AI, automation, and business strategy

Just like cyber, the AI service portfolio will mature and multiply.

I don't have a crystal ball, but I can safely say that a wave of AI services that are geared toward the MSP channel will appear.

There will be opportunities to resell these services, build more advanced services and continue to grow.

Where to Go From Here

So what *should* you build next?

Here is a series of forward-leaning AI services to consider layering in:

AI Operations Consulting

Help clients document repeatable processes that can be enhanced by AI or automation. Think of it as vAIO meets process reengineering.

Custom GPT Builds and Copilot Agents

Building custom GPT for departments like HR, sales, or support. Building Copilot agents that automate workflows.

Prompt Library Subscriptions

Maintain updated prompt packs by role. Bundle these with usage training and feedback loops.

AI Performance Reviews

Monthly or quarterly reviews of top AI use cases, productivity wins, risks flagged, and new opportunities.

Automation Layering

Use Zapier, Make, Power Automate, and Copilot studio to connect AI tools with existing platforms (e.g., CRM → AI summary → Teams/email alert).

AI Policy & Governance Audits

Review clients' AI usage, tools, and risks. Help update Acceptable Use Policies and security controls.

AI Champions Program

Identify and train internal champions at client organizations to lead AI adoption from within.

Industry-Specific AI Playbooks

Build templated playbooks for industries you serve: dental, legal, healthcare, real estate, and so on.

New AI Tool Evaluations

Guide clients on new tools, features and functionalities

These are natural progression of vAIO services your MSP can be well-positioned to offer clients.

Building Your AI Team: Skills, Resources, and Evolution

Here is something you may be wondering about:

> "Do I need new people? New skills?
> Or can my current team handle this?"

Fair question.

And here's the honest answer: *Maybe.*

AI services aren't pure tech services like firewalls or backup solutions.

They're not "install and forget" like traditional MSP offerings.

The skills needed for advanced AI services require the ability to analyze client workflows and identify improvement opportunities. You need deeper interaction with clients to understand how they actually work, not just what technology they use.

You'll build automations and integrations that connect AI tools with existing business systems. You must understand business processes across departments, sales, marketing, HR, finance, not just IT infrastructure. And you need to think strategically about productivity optimization and process improvement.

That's different from configuring a firewall or managing patches.

Your AI Evangelists Are Already Here

Here's the good news: Some of your employees will naturally evolve these skills. Especially the employees who are already using AI and believe in its potential.

They'll become your internal evangelists.

They'll be the ones who get excited about helping clients optimize workflows.

They'll naturally gravitate toward the process analysis and automation thinking that AI services require.

Watch for these employees:

- They're already experimenting with AI tools
- They ask questions about client business processes
- They think beyond "fix the problem" to "how can we improve this?"
- They enjoy training and explaining concepts to others

These are your future AI service leads.

New Skills, New Opportunities

As your AI practice grows, you'll likely need to add capabilities:

- **Process analysts** who can map client workflows and identify automation opportunities
- **Automation builders** who can connect AI tools with existing business systems
- **Client success managers** who can guide ongoing AI adoption and optimization

Some of these skills will come from within.

Others might require new hires.

The Channel Partner Option

Just like with cybersecurity, you don't have to build everything in-house. Channel-friendly vendors are already emerging who offer advanced AI services—think of them as the MSSPs of the AI world.

They'll handle the complex automations, custom agent builds, training at scale, and deep workflow integrations.

You'll maintain the client relationship and strategic oversight.

This is probably where most MSPs will land: owning the strategy, but partnering for the complexity.

Don't Overthink It

Just like it's hard to see where AI is going past the next six months, it's hard to predict exactly what skillsets you'll need.

But that's okay.

Start with what you have.

Use your current team to deliver training, policies, and basic AI enablement.

As clients' needs evolve, your team will evolve.

As advanced services become necessary, the market will provide solutions.

The key is starting now, with the resources you have, rather than waiting for perfect clarity about what you'll need later.

Your team's AI skills will grow alongside your clients' AI adoption. That's how it's always worked.

That's how it'll work with AI too.

FINAL WORD

THIS IS ONLY THE BEGINNING

If you've made it this far, you're ready.

The MSPs who act now will own the next decade.

While others wait for clarity, you'll be building expertise.

While competitors debate readiness, you'll be delivering results.

While consultants chase your clients, you'll already own the relationship.

You've done this before.

Cloud. Security. Compliance.

Every time, you guided clients through the chaos.

Every time, you turned complexity into clarity.

Every time, you won.

AI is no different.

Except bigger. Faster. More valuable.

Your clients are using AI today—with or without you.

The question isn't whether AI will transform their businesses.

The question is whether you'll lead that transformation.

Start small today.

Build trust tomorrow.

Own the future.

Lead like you always have.

EXCLUSIVE READER OFFER

Start leading AI conversations today!

Ready to implement what you've learned? Get the tools and credibility to position your MSP as the AI leader your clients need.

Claim Your Exclusive Package

FREE 30-Day BSN Trial:

- Complete AI Awareness Training platform – ready to deliver to clients immediately

- Implementation Toolkit AI adoption playbooks, policy templates, prompt libraries, and client conversation scripts

- Generative AI Certification – Industry-first MSP certification to showcase your AI expertise and differentiate from consultants

---

TAKE ACTION NOW

www.breachsecurenow.com/FromPromptToProfit

You have everything you need to become your clients' trusted AI advisor starting today.

Questions?

Email: **success@breachsecurenow.com**

AFTERWORD

A PERSONAL NOTE

Thank you for reading my book.

This wasn't written by an AI analyst or ghostwritten by a tech journalist. Although ChatGPT and Claude did assist with the writing, the thoughts, experiences, and insights came from me—an MSP owner, CEO of Breach Secure Now, and someone who's been in this industry for over 25 years.

I've watched every major technology wave transform our industry: the internet, the cloud, cybersecurity, compliance.

Every time, the pattern is the same:

- First, it seems too early
- Then, it feels too risky
- Then, it becomes obvious
- And finally, it's too late to lead

AI is right between those last two phases.

It's obvious that AI will transform how businesses operate. And it's still early enough for you to lead that transformation.

That's why I wrote this. Not to scare you. Not to overhype the tools. But to help you see the real opportunity in front of you—as an MSP, as a leader, and as someone your clients already trust.

The Starting Line, Not the Finish

I fully expect someone to read this book in 2-3 years and chuckle to themselves about how simple AI was in 2025.

In fact, I'd be disappointed if that wasn't the case. Because if AI isn't dramatically more powerful and integrated by then, we'll have missed the AI revolution entirely.

But here's my hope... that this book helps thousands of MSPs start their AI journey today. And that those MSPs go on to help hundreds of thousands of SMB clients and millions of employees utilize AI in a safe and effective manner.

That's the real goal. Not to predict the future perfectly, but to help you position yourself to ride every wave that comes next.

Why I Believe in MSPs

You've always been the steady hand guiding clients through technological chaos.

When the internet felt overwhelming, you made it manageable.

When the cloud seemed risky, you made it secure.

When cybersecurity became essential, you made it understandable.

Now your clients are adopting AI without a plan, without policies, and without understanding the risks.

That's both dangerous and your biggest opportunity.

You don't need to become an AI engineer.

You just need to do what you've always done: bring clarity to complexity.

What I Hope You'll Do Next

Start using AI in your own business. Experience it firsthand.

Then help one client at a time:

- Start conversations about AI risks and opportunities
- Offer training that protects them while enabling productivity

- Help create policies that encourage safe experimentation

- Find quick wins that build confidence and momentum

If you're not ready to do everything at once, just do one thing.

Progress beats perfection.

On the way to optimal is suboptimal.

My Commitment to You

At Breach Secure Now, we're building the platform to help MSPs lead the AI transformation—just like we did with cybersecurity awareness.

We're committed to providing:

- Real-world AI training content you can deliver to clients

- Tools that make AI conversations easier to start

- MSP AI certifications and bootcamps

- Resources that help clients adopt AI safely and productively

- Frameworks for building lasting AI service practices

The MSPs who start now will define the next decade of our industry.

Your clients need a trusted guide through the AI transformation. You've been that guide before. You can be that guide again.

Let's lead this together.

—**Art Gross**
CEO, Breach Secure Now

About the Author

ART GROSS is a serial entrepreneur and the CEO of Breach Secure Now, a leading provider of human-centric cybersecurity, AI awareness, and HIPAA compliance training for Managed Service Providers (MSPs). Known for building mission-driven companies with strong, people-first cultures, Art has spent over four decades at the intersection of technology, security, and healthcare.

He began his career as a Corporate Systems Architect at Merck & Co., Inc., and in 2000 founded Entegration, Inc., which he continues to lead today. Entegration provides IT services to healthcare organizations, including some of the largest fertility practices in the world.

In 2010, Art launched Breach Secure Now to help MSPs address the human side of cybersecurity and manage HIPAA compliance. In 2024, the company expanded its mission to include productivity training, introducing Microsoft 365 and AI awareness programs to help employees work more securely and effectively.

He also founded HIPAA Secure Now to help medical practices comply with HIPAA regulations and protect patient information, and Inskyber to provide cyber insurance solutions for MSPs and their clients.

Art holds a B.S. in Computer Science from Penn State University and an MBA in Management from Fairleigh Dickinson University. His leadership continues to shape how MSPs build trust, strengthen security, and help businesses become more productive in today's complex technology environment.

Made in the USA
Las Vegas, NV
03 August 2025

25779705R00094